GURU GOBIND SINGH MARG

AS VISUALISED BY ARTIST TRILOK SINGH

HARPAL KAUR & JOTINDER SINGH

White Falcon Publishing

www.whitefalconpublishing.com

Guru Gobind Singh Marg
as visualised by Artist Trilok Singh

Harpal Kaur & Jotinder Singh

www.whitefalconpublishing.com

First Edition, 2020

The contents of this book have been timestamped on the Ethereum blockchain as a permanent proof of existence. Scan the QR code or visit the URL given on the back cover to verify the blockchain certification for this book.

ISBN - 978-93-89530-78-0

The book available at:-

India - Chitralok Patiala(Pb) 147001 S. Jotinder Singh Mob. 9779915525, email jotinder412@gmail.com
- WFP stores. whitefalconpublish@gmail.com

Online - Amazon, Flipkart. Search→Author name/Book name
- Ebooks on Amazon Kindle. Search→Author name/Book name

Canada - Hardarshan Memorial International Trust, Surrey, BC. S. Jaiteg Singh Anant Mob. 778-385-8141 email jaiteganant@yahoo.com

United Kingdom - Bhai Randhir Singh Trust, Stafford S. Jujhar Singh 755-471-1133.

Guru Gobind Singh Marg as visualised by Artist Trilok Singh

All the paintings and Guru Gobind Singh marg (route map) work by

S. Trilok Singh Artist (1914-1990),
'Chitralok', Chitralok marg, Arjan nagar, near Modi College, Patiala. 147001 Punjab.

Website www.triloksinghartist.com
Wikipedia- Trilok Singh Chitarkar

Text Written by
1. Ms. Harpal Kaur
   MA(English). B.ed.
2. S. Jotinder Singh S/o late S. Trilok Singh Artist

Engineer-in Chief/Retd PSEB 2006,
Consultant Power Finance Corporation (GoI) for development of
Thermal Projects & transmission of power in Punjab 2007-08 &
Consultant to 1980 MW Talwandi Sabo Super Critical Thermal Power Project,
Mansa (Punjab) 2008-2016

Address;- 'Chitralok', Chitralok marg, Arjan nagar, near Modi College, Patiala. 147001 Punjab

Painting page designed by
S. Jotinder Singh S/o late S. Trilok Singh Artist

Edited by
S. Amrik Singh Executive Engineer/ Irrigation Punjab -Retd
AMIE, MA(History), MA (English) & MA(Religion),
Director, Atma Devi Public High School, Morinda. Distt. Ropar (Punjab)

Special Thanks *to our beloved daughter Dr. Upinder Kaur, M.S (Ophthalmology) and family, son Er. Hemjeet Singh ME(Civil) and family without whose support and encouragement it would not have been possible to write this book.*

ਦੇਹ ਸਿਵਾ ਬਰੁ ਮੋਹਿ ਇਹੈ ਸੁਭ ਕਰਮਨ ਤੇ ਕਬਹੂੰ ਨ ਟਰੋਂ।।
ਨਾ ਡਰੋਂ ਅਰਿ ਸੋ ਜਬ ਜਾਇ ਲਰੋਂ ਨਿਸਚੈ ਕਰ ਅਪੁਨੀ ਜੀਤ ਕਰੋਂ।।
ਅਰੁ ਸਿਖ ਹੋਂ ਆਪਨੇ ਹੀ ਮਨ ਕੌ ਇਹ ਲਾਲਚ ਹਉ ਗੁਨ ਤਉ ਉਚਰੋਂ।
ਜਬ ਆਵ ਕੀ ਅਉਧ ਨਿਦਾਨ ਬਨੈ ਅਤਿ ਹੀ ਰਨ ਮੈ ਤਬ ਜੂਝ ਮਰੋਂ।।

O God, grant me this boon that I may never ever shirk from doing good deeds.
I shall not fear from combat and with determination achieve victory.
I may instruct my mind to always utter God's praise.
When this mortal life comes to end, I may die
fighting courageously for noble cause.

- *Guru Gobind Singh*

(May–1990)

This book is dedicated to my loving parents
S. Trilok Singh Artist (1914-1990) and Harbans Kaur (1920-1990)

ਮਿਤ੍ਰ ਪਿਆਰੇ ਨੂੰ ਹਾਲ ਮੁਰੀਦਾਂ ਦਾ ਕਹਿਣਾ।
ਤੁਧੁ ਬਿਨੁ ਰੋਗ ਰਜਾਈਆਂ ਦਾ ਓਢਣ ਨਾਗ ਨਿਵਾਸਾਂ ਦੇ ਰਹਿਣਾ।
ਸੂਲ ਸੁਰਾਹੀ ਖੰਜਰੁ ਪਿਆਲਾ ਬਿੰਗ ਕਸਾਈਆਂ ਦਾ ਸਹਿਣਾ।
ਯਾਰੜੇ ਦਾ ਸਾਨੂੰ ਸਥਰ ਚੰਗਾ ਭੱਠ ਖੇੜਿਆਂ ਦਾ ਰਹਿਣਾ॥

Tell the Beloved Friend of the plight of His followers
Without Him, the comfort of soft beds is a disease.
Comforts of life in palaces is like living with snakes.
The pitcher of wine is a thorn and the cup like a dagger.
Without Him, Life is a butcher's knife itself.
The Guru in this Shabad yearns for remembrance of WaheGuru
despite extreme hardship & tough times rather than living
comfortably without WaheGuru's name.

CONTENTS

GURU GOBIND SINGH MARG

(Anandpur Sahib to Talwandi Sabo)

INTRODUCTION

Guru Gobind Singh Marg is the route taken by the Tenth Guru, *Sahibe-e-Kamal* Guru Gobind Singh from Anandpur Sahib to Talwandi Sabo covering about 640KMs. This Marg is blessed by the sacred touch of the Tenth Guru's feet and supreme sacrifices of Sikh warriors while fighting with combined forces of Hill-Rajas and Mughals. This Marg has got a very significant place in the history of Sikhs and Punjab. The Guru transformed the lives of the people on the way and instilled courage and new energy in the lives of the people.

All the paintings included in the book are by my father Sardar Trilok Singh Artist (1914-1990). My father had prepared the map of Guru Gobind Singh Marg with illustrations showing all the places visited on the way and blessed by the Tenth Guru. This was published by the Language Department, Punjab in 1973.

Guru Gobind Singh Marg was inaugurated on April 10, 1973 at a state-level function at Anandpur Sahib by the then Chief Minister of Punjab - Giani Zail Singh amidst great rejoicing and fanfare. A Mahan Yatra started from Anandpur on April 10, 1973 and reached Damdama Sahib on Baisakhi, April 13, 1973. This highway was constructed, connecting 91 shrines and twenty Dashmesh pentagonal pillars on the route with the inscriptions of the sacred verses/teachings of the great Guru in Punjabi, Hindi, English and Urdu.

Guru Gobind Singh was a spiritual leader, poet par excellence, scholar, philosopher, fearless warrior, supreme commander, *Sarbans Dani* who sacrificed everything he had for the sake of protecting and uplifting weaker sections of society and fighting against injustice and tyranny. A Muslim poet Alha Yaar Khan has written that there is no one equivalent to Guru Gobind Singh. (ਇਨਸਾਫ਼ ਕਰੇ ਜੀ ਮੇਂ ਜ਼ਮਾਨਾ ਤੋ ਯਕੀਂ ਹੈ, ਕਹ ਦੇ ਗੁਰੂ ਗੋਬਿੰਦ ਕਾ ਸਾਨੀ ਹੀ ਨਹੀਂ ਹੈ।)

Guru Gobind Singh, the Tenth Guru of the Sikhs called himself a mere servant of the Supreme Lord who has come to witness the drama of life, (ਮੈ ਹੋ ਪਰਮ ਪੁਰਖ ਕੋ ਦਾਸਾ ......) was born at Patna Sahib (Bihar) in 1666 while his father Guru Teg Bahadur was on a missionary tour to Eastern states. That day, Pir Bhikhan Shah in Punjab performed his prayer towards East direction instead of Makka situated in west, telling his disciples that God has revealed himself in the form of a newborn in Patna. The Pir reached Patna to pay obeisance to Gobind Rai. The Pir held out two bowls containing milk and water separately - symbolic of Hinduism and Islam. Gobind Rai touched both and smiled.

In *Bachitar Natak*, an autobiography of the Tenth Guru, his mission is very clear:-

ਯਾਹੀ ਕਾਜ ਧਰਾ ਹਮ ਜਨਮੰ	I have taken birth for this purpose
ਸਮਝ ਲੇਹੁ ਸਾਧੂ ਸਭ ਮਨਮੰ।	Let all the holy men understand this in their minds
ਧਰਮ ਚਲਾਵਨ ਸੰਤ ਉਬਾਰਨ	I have come to spread Dharma and protecting saints
ਦੁਸਟ ਸਭਨ ਕੋ ਮੂਲ ਉਪਾਰਨ।।	and for uprooting the tyrants.

Gobind Rai spent about five years of his life in Patna Sahib. Guru Teg Bahadur met Gobind Rai at Patna Sahib on his return from the missionary tour. He could not spend much time with his family at Patna Sahib and returned to Anandpur Sahib. Later on, the family along with Gobind Rai joined him at Anandpur Sahib. Gobind Rai devoted his time to study Persian, Arabic, Sanskirt, Brij and Indian classics and also getting trained in horse riding and martial arts.

The forcible conversion of religion started vigorously in Kashmir. A deputation of Kashmiri Pandits came to seek the help of Guru Teg Bahadur at Anandpur. The Guru felt that only a sacrifice by a holy person can stop this conversion. Everybody became pensive. Gobind Rai, who was just nine years old, entered the room at that time and enquired about the problem and spontaneously said that there was none more pious than the Guru himself. The Guru advised the Pandits to tell Emperor Aurangzeb that they were ready to embrace Islam if Guru Teg Bahadur first accepts Islam. Nominating Gobind Rai as his successor, Guru Teg Bahadur left for Delhi. There, the Guru refused to accept Islam or perform miracle. Aurangzeb passed orders to execute the Guru and his disciples. On November 11, 1675, the Guru was beheaded subsequently after martyrdom of his three disciples Bhai Mati Dass, Dayal Dass and Sati Dass for the sake of Dharma and is righteously known as '*Srishti Di Chadar*' - protector of other religion.

Bhai Jaita picked up Guru Teg Bahadur's beheaded head and brought it to Anandpur Sahib. The body was taken by Lakhi Shah Banjara, a local Sikh merchant, who cremated the body, by burning his house completely. Gurdwara Rakabganj exists at that place.

On receiving Bhai Jaita with Guru Teg Bahadur's head, Guru Gobind Singh showed immense courage and maturity and said *Rangreta Guru ka beta* (ਰੰਘਰੇਟਾ ਗੁਰੂ ਕਾ ਬੇਟਾ).

From centuries, the Hindu society was divided into castes. The Upper caste had the monopoly of education, religious reading, teaching and were custodians of religion, whereas, the lowest caste were the untouchables and had no rights except to serve other castes. The Muslims came as invaders, took advantage of the society and began to establish their own regime. The ruling class began a reign of injustice and persecution. Muslim rulers had imposed Jazia tax on others.

The first Guru, Guru Nanak Dev came to the world in 1469 and wrote in *Majh Ki Var* that age is like a knife, Rajas are butchers, religion has taken wings and flown (...ਕਲਿ ਕਾਤਿ ਰਾਜੇ ਕਾਸਾਈ ਧਰਮੁ ਪੰਖ ਕਰਿ ਉਡਰਿਆ). He travelled to various places and countries to spread his message of *Ek Onkar* - (ੴ) means there is one God. All human beings are equal before the Almighty God (ਏਕ ਪਿਤਾ ਏਕਸ ਕੇ ਹਮ ਬਾਰਿਕ). The message continued to be spread by the successive Gurus.

For the next 10 years from 1675-1685, Guru Gobind Singh devoted himself educating, motivating and guiding the people in the turbulent times. He wanted to inculcate the feeling of brotherhood, equality in the minds of the people. 'Fear not and Frighten not' (ਭੈ ਕਾਹੂ ਕੋ ਦੇਤ ਨਹਿ ...।) was always his motto. The Guru had the determination to fight the atrocities of the Mughal Empire and the willpower to help the downtrodden classes of the society. He prepared himself for this most difficult task before him. For the Guru, all the human beings are the children of the same Almighty God. People rich or poor, belonging to different castes and creed were equal in his eyes (ਹਿੰਦੂ ਤੁਰਕ ਕੋਊ ਰਾਫਜੀ ਇਮਾਮ ਸਾਫੀ ਮਾਨਸ ਕੀ ਜਾਤਿ ਸਬੈ ਏਕੈ ਪਹਿਚਾਨਬੋ।।). He prepared an integrated society and infused the spirit of humanism, fearlessness and the willpower to fight the atrocities and tyrannies of rulers. He prepared Ranjit Nagara and used it in expeditions. He started giving training to Sikhs. Being the spiritual head, people started coming from all directions. Different castes began to sit together, taking food together, getting horse training, learning war tactics, martial activities, mock exercises, and education.

The Hill-Rajas were watching all of this in awe. The splendour of the Guru, formation of an integrated society, lower classes getting spiritual teachings, performing martial activities disturbed them. The situation was averted when Medni Prakash, Hill-Raja of Sirmur invited the Guru to his state Nahan. The Guru accepted his invitation and he liked the scenic beauty of the area and spent some time there. He settled at Paonta Sahib on the banks of river Yamuna. This was the most peaceful and creative time spent by the Guru. 52 poets were in his poetic court. Most of his valuable compositions were written here and literature of Indian mythology was translated into simple language of the people. All these have been preserved in Dasam Granth. He inspired his young devotees and followers to be trained in martial activity for the benefit of society. He also welcomed able-bodied men to join him to fight against the tyranny of rulers and protect the weaker ones. Growing power of the Guru was not acceptable to Hill-Rajas, thus it led to a fierce battle of Bhangani near Paonta Sahib and the Guru became victorious in the first battle imposed by the Hill-Rajas on him. The Guru has written about this battle in Bachitar Natak where he thanked the Almighty for this victory. Pir Budhu Shah, a Muslim saint of Sadhaura (near Yamunanagar) helped the Guru during this battle. He sent about 500 men to fight for the Guru. His two sons and about 200 disciples were also killed in the battle helping the Guru.

After the battle of Bhangani, the Guru shifted back to Anandpur Sahib. When Mughal forces attacked the rulers of Kangra and Bilaspur for not paying tax, the cunning Hill-Rajas sought the help of the Guru. With the help of the Guru, the Mughals were defeated in the battle of Nadaun in 1687. For better defence of Anandpur Sahib, the Guru built forts (Anandgarh, Lohgarh, Keshgarh, Fatehgarh) on the strategic places. Many battles were fought and all were won by the Sikhs. The Guru abolished the earlier established system of *Masands* (Religious agents of Sikh Gurus to collect offerings) as they had become corrupt with the passage of time. The devotees were asked to come directly to Anandpur Sahib.

The Guru resolved to complete the work started by the first Guru to transform the community into saint-soldiers. The Baisakhi of 1699 of Anandpur Sahib holds a special place in the history when the Guru asked his followers to attend Baisakhi day at Anandpur Sahib. On this historic day, the Guru with naked sword in hand, appeared before the large gathering of about 80,000 people from all over India and demanded the head of one person. The audience became dumbfounded and some even left the *Pandal*. On the second call by the Guru, Daya Ram of Lahore came forward and offered his head. The Guru took him inside the tent and again came back with sword dripping with blood and demanded the head of another person. This happened four times more and four men - Dharam Das from Hastinapur, Himmat Rai from Jagannath, Mohkam Chand from Dawarka and Sahib Chand from Bidar offered their heads. They were all taken to the tent. Then the Guru prepared *Amrit*. The Guru bapitised them with *Amrit* and called them *Panj Pyare (*five beloved ones) - named as Khalsa and they were given authority to baptise others and take decision collectively in difficult situations. After baptising them, the Guru also got baptised by them and became Gobind Singh from Gobind Rai. Guru Gobind Singh merged in the same brotherhood and became the Guru as well as the disciple. (ਵਾਹੁ ਵਾਹੁ ਗੋਬਿੰਦ ਸਿੰਘ ਆਪੇ ਗੁਰ ਚੇਲਾ).

On the same day, thousands of other devotees and followers were baptised. From then, all were to carry the surname; men as SINGH and women as KAUR and take five emblems of brotherhood; *Kesh* (uncut hair), *Kangha* (comb), *Kara* (a steel bracelet), *Kachha* (short breeches) and *Kirpan* (sword). The baptism was the rebirth of all into a new family of brotherhood, a new *Panth* called *Khalsa*. They all became equal in caste and creed and sons and daughters of Guru Gobind Singh and Mata Sahib Kaur. All in a loud voice gave a rousing applause of *Waheguru ji ka khalsa Waheguru ji ki Fateh* (The *Khalsa* belongs to the Glorious God and the God is victorious). On meeting, they greet each other with the same applause. With this, the Guru created a new breed of *Saint-*Soldiers (ਸੰਤ ਸਿਪਾਹੀਆਂ ਦੀ ਫ਼ੌਜ) who were prepared to lay down their lives to defend the weaker section and fight against the injustice. They were daring, truthful, dedicated, and devoted to the Guru and ready to sacrifice for Dharma.

But all this did not go well with Hill-Rajas. They attacked Anandpur Sahib many times but could not succeed. The continuous defeats had shattered the confidence of the Hill-Rajas. The Hill-Rajas collectively brought forth an armoured, intoxicated elephant to batter at the main gate of Lohgarh fort at Anandpur Sahib. Bhai Bachittar Singh was tasked by the Guru to fight the elephant with a *Nagni Barcha*, a type of spear. As the elephant approached the gate, Bhai Bachitar Singh sallied forth on horseback and made a powerful thrust with his spear piercing the elephant's armour plate and injuring the animal in the forehead. This compelled the elephant to turn back swinging its trunk with sword left and right cutting through their soldiers and trampling them under its feet. The Hill- Rajas were stunned and shaken.

The Hill-Rajas complained to Aurangzeb about the Guru's rising power and asked for his help. They offered to pay the expenses for the Mughal army. Aurangzeb sent huge armies from Sarhind and other provinces to tackle the Guru. The combined forces barricaded Anandpur Sahib and attacked many times. Barricaded skirmishes continued but the Sikhs managed to defeat them. The combined forces of Hill-Rajas and Mughals regrouped and laid complete siege to Anandpur Sahib for about seven months, they could not defeat the Khalsa forces and could not force the Khalsa to vacate Anandpur Sahib. Then, the combined forces of Hill-Rajas and Mughals on the oath taken on the Quran, cow and Holybook, requested the Guru to vacate Anandpur Sahib and assured that they would not harm anybody. The Guru could not see the sufferings of his people and vacated Anandpur Sahib in the company of his family and Sikhs on December 20, 1704.

As soon as they left Anandpur Sahib, the combined forces of Hill-Rajas and Mughals forgot all about the oaths and promises. They chased and attacked the Guru. Bhai Udey Singh (s/o Bhai Mani Singh) along with 50 Sikhs accepted the orders of the

Guru to restrict advancement of the attacking forces near Shahi Tibbi. They defended bravely and all attained martyrdom after killing many of them. The Guru reached the bank of Sirsa river but the river was in full spate, the chasing combined forces also started gathering. Here the responsibility to restrict the movement of combined forces was left to Bhai Jiwan Singh accompanied by 100 Sikhs. They kept the forces at bay. A fierce battle took place. They restricted the movement of combined forces for about six hours and many Sikhs attained martyrdom. After completing the recitation of *Aasa Di Var* on the banks of river Sirsa peacefully, the Guru, the family and the remaining Sikhs crossed the river Sirsa.

While crossing the Sirsa river, Mata Gujari and younger Sahibzadas got separated from the Guru. Mata Sundri and Mata Sahib Kaur left for Delhi with Bhai Mani Singh and a few Sikhs. The Guru directed Bhai Bachittar Singh, Sahibzada Ajit Singh and Jujhar Singh and about 100 Sikhs to reach village Kotla Nihang Khan via Malikpur, a village of Muslim Ranghars. The Ranghar Muslims of Malikpur, attacked the group of Sikhs led by Bhai Bachittar Singh and a fierce fight took place there. In the combat, many Sikhs laid down their lives. Bhai Bachittar Singh was wounded seriously. He was taken to the Haveli of Nihang Khan and was left in his care. Then the Guru and Sikhs went towards Chamkaur Sahib.

The Guru stationed himself in the mud-built Haveli at Chamkaur Sahib. About 10 lakh combined forces of Hill-Rajas and Mughals, who had chased the Guru earnestly, also reached there. Next day, there began one of the unique and rare battles in the history of mankind - 40 famished Sikhs without any proper weapons had to fight the 10 lakh combined forces. Sikhs went out in small batches of five, fought valiantly, killing hundreds of soldiers and attained martyrdom before laying down their lives and kept them engaged throughout the day. Sahibzada Ajit Singh and Jujhar Singh also fought bravely and killed hundreds of soldiers before laying down their lives. Guru observed them from the top of the Haveli and thanked the Almighty God. By evening, when only a few Sikhs were left in the Haveli, they passed the *Gurmata* (Resolution) and commanded the Guru to leave Chamkaur Sahib for the sake of *Khalsa*. The Guru, Bhai Man Singh, Daya Singh and Dharam Singh left the Haveli in the dark night. While going out, the Guru clapped three times and said *Pir-e-Hind Mey Rawad* (The Guru is going - ਪੀਰੇ ਹਿੰਦ ਮੇ ਰਵੱਦ). All of them left in different directions and the Guru walked towards Machhiwara.

During the day, the Guru slept in the thicket of trees and covered the distance during the night. He reached a garden near Machhiwara and slept there. Here he composed the hymn *Mitre pyare nu*... (ਮਿਤ੍ਰ ਪਿਆਰੇ ਨੂੰ ਹਾਲ ਮੁਰੀਦਾਂ ਦਾ ਕਹਿਣਾ...). While searching for the Guru, Bhai Man Singh, Daya Singh and Dharam Singh also reached there. Gulaba,

INTRODUCTION

a *masand*, owner of the garden took them to his house and served them food. Gani Khan and Nabi Khan, two Rohilla Pathans who used to bring horses for the Guru, came to know and took the Guru to their residence respectfully. They dressed the Guru as '*Uch Da Pir*'. Nabi Khan, Gani Khan, Bhai Dharam Singh, Daya Singh and Man Singh carried the *Manji* (palanquin) and further marched from there. Meanwhile, the combined forces became aware of the Guru's escape. They started door to door search for the Guru.

On the way, checking forces of Mughals stopped them for verification/identification. Quazi Pir Mohammad, a Maulvi who had taught Persian to the Guru, identified the Guru as 'Uch Da Pir'. After that, they were allowed to go further. Crossing many villages on the way, they reached Alamgir. Here Bhai Nauddh Singh brought a horse for the Guru. The Guru discarded the palanquin shouldered by them. The Guru gave Hukamnama describing Gani Khan and Nabi Khan as Guru's *Farzands* (sons). From here, the Guru moved towards Raikot. Here Rai Kalha welcomed him and offered help. The Guru asked Rai Kalha to send someone to know about the fate of the younger sons and Mata Gujri. Noora Mahi, a servant of Rai Kalha went to Sarhind and brought the news about how the younger Sahibzadas were bricked alive and Mata Gujri had also passed away. The Guru thanked the Almighty God and predicted the doom of the tyrant Mughal Empire.

From there, halting at many places, the Guru reached Dina-Kangar. Here the Guru lived for a few days and from here, he wrote Zaffarnama - 'the Epistle of Victory' to Aurangzeb. In the letter of victory to Aurangzeb, the Guru happily justified the battle and wrote that when all the means for justice have failed and no hope is in sight, it is then rightful to take up sword (ਚੂੰ ਕਾਰ ਅਜ਼ ਹਮਾਂ ਹੀਲਤੇ ਦਰ ਗੁਜ਼ੱਸ਼ਤ। ਹਲਾਲ ਅਸਤ ਬੁਰਦਨ ਬ ਸ਼ਮਸ਼ੀਰ ਦਸਤ।). The 'sword' symbolising *Shakti* was not to be used as a butcher's knife but as a surgeon's instrument to root out the tyrannies. The Guru did not fight any battle for name, fame, wealth or any territory but fought against the tyranny imposed by the Hill-Rajas and Mughal rulers. All the battles fought by the Guru during his lifetime were for the betterment of downtrodden people. The Guru sent Bhai Daya Singh and Dharam Singh to deliver the letter to Aurangzeb, who was in Deccan (South India). Then the Guru moved towards Kotkapura.

The Guru came to know that Wazir Khan, the Governor of Sarhind was chasing him. He wanted some proper place to tackle him. By that time, the Guru had many volunteer Sikhs and paid soldiers had also assembled around the Guru. The Guru moved ahead and reached Khidrana. Wazir Khan with his strong army also reached there. Forty Sikhs, who had left the Guru at Anandpur Sahib also came back under the leadership of Mai Bhago and a fierce battle was fought there between Sikhs and Mughal forces.

The Guru saw the battle from the top of a mound. He attacked Mughal forces with arrows. The Mughal forces were compelled to go back. The Guru came to the battlefield and found Mahan Singh, leader of 40 deserters who had laid down their lives there, still alive. The Guru sat down and placed Mahan Singh's head in his lap and asked him if he had any wish to be fulfilled. Mahan Singh asked the Guru to tear off the *Bedaba* - a denouncement letter signed by them. Guru took it out from under his belt and tore it off. He called all the forty Sikhs as Muktas. The Guru himself performed the last rites of these Sikhs. This place is now known as Mukatsar.

The Guru continued his journey towards Malwa area and reached Talwandi Sabo. He stayed there for about nine months. Bhai Dalla, a true devotee of the Guru welcomed him. Mata Sundri, Mata Sahib Kaur and Bhai Mani Singh joined the Guru there. On enquiring about their sons, the Guru replied that he had sacrificed his four sons for the sake of Khalsa. So what, if four are dead but thousands are still alive (ਇਨ ਪੁਤਰਨ ਕੇ ਸੀਸ ਪਰ ਵਾਰ ਦੀਏ ਸੁਤ ਚਾਰ। ਚਾਰ ਮੁਏ ਤੋ ਕਿਆ ਹੁਆ ਜੀਵਤ ਕਈ ਹਜਾਰ।). It was here the Guru dictated the whole of Guru Granth Sahib and got it written as the authorised version of *Adi Granth* and added the Bani of Guru Teg Bahadur. Bhai Mani Singh wrote it and Baba Deep Singh made four copies of the Granth for the four Takhats. The place became a gathering place for the scholars just like Anandpur Sahib. It has come to be known as *Guru ki Kashi*.

Till then, Guru had not heard from the Emperor Aurangzeb, so he set out towards Deccan (South India). But on the way, he came to know about the death of Aurangzeb. A war of succession immediately broke out among the Mughal princes. Muazzam Shah, who was later known as Bahadur Shah, sought Guru's help. The Guru helped him to become the Emperor. Bahadur Shah invited the Guru to Delhi, offered him robes of honour and other presents. Later on, the Guru went towards Deccan (South India) along with the Emperor up to Hyderabad via Agra.

When the Guru became sure that Bahadur Shah was not inclined to take any action against Sarhind ruler Wazir Khan, he separated from the Emperor. Then, the Guru went towards river Godavari, presently, known as Nanded Sahib. He met a *Bairagi Sadhu* Madho Das there, who later became Banda Singh (Gurbax Singh after baptising by the Guru). The Guru gave Banda Singh five arrows, a Nagara, Hukamnamas, a few Sikhs and blessed him with a specific task to tackle the Sarhind ruler, Wazir Khan. Banda Singh came to Punjab like a whirlwind and defeated the one lakh forces by mere 15000 volunteers. Wazir Khan was killed in the battle at Chapar chiri and brought to Sarhind, tied and dragged by the horse. Banda Singh Bahadur established the first Sikh Raj and minted the coins in the name of the Gurus.

After sending Banda Singh to Punjab, the Guru stayed at Nanded Sahib. Two Pathans were sent earlier by Wazir Khan, Governor of Sarhind to kill the Guru. One of them attacked the Guru with a dagger. The wound proved to be a fatal one. The Guru killed the attacker Pathan with his dagger. The other Pathan was killed by the Sikhs while he was running away. When the Guru sensed his physical end is near, he declared and installed the Guru Granth Sahib as the Guru of the Sikhs. He ordered the Sikhs to revere and to bow before the Guru Granth Sahib. It contains the spirit of all the Gurus.

ਸਭ ਸਿੱਖਨ ਕੋ ਹੁਕਮ ਹੈ, ਗੁਰੂ ਮਾਨਿਓ ਗ੍ਰੰਥ।
ਗੁਰੂ ਗ੍ਰੰਥ ਜੀ ਮਾਨਿਓ, ਪ੍ਰਗਟ ਗੁਰਾਂ ਕੀ ਦੇਹ।।

In the short span of his charismatic life, Guru Gobind Singh achieved the near impossible mission. He brought miraculous transformation in the people and he infused such a spirit in the weaker sections that they were ready to lay down their lives at the altar of truth. He made them fearless, courageous, truthful human beings - true saint soldiers. He sacrificed everything he had for the betterment of the people and Khalsa. He had faith in the *Akal Purkh* and believed all men are equal in the eyes of the God. He loved every one irrespective of caste, creed, social status or any other man-made distinctions - (ਸਾਚੁ ਕਹੋਂ ਸੁਨ ਲਹੋ ਸਭੈ, ਜਿਨ ਪ੍ਰੇਮ ਕੀਓ, ਤਿਨ ਹੀ ਪ੍ਰਭ ਪਾਇਓ।।).

Hakim Alha Yaar Khan Yogi has beautifully written about Guru Gobind Singh in 1915 that all praise of the Guru is insufficient:-

ਕਰਤਾਰ ਕੀ ਸੌਗੰਦ ਹੈ ਨਾਨਕ ਕੀ ਕਸਮ ਹੈ।
ਜਿਤਨੀ ਭੀ ਹੋ ਗੋਬਿੰਦ ਕੀ ਤਾਰੀਫ ਵੁਹ ਕਮ ਹੈ।।

Jotinder Singh
Engineer-in-Chief/Retd
Chitralok, Patiala

INTRODUCTION

ਨਾਸਰੋ ਮਨਸੂਰ ਗੁਰੁ ਗੋਬਿੰਦ ਸਿੰਘ॥ ਏਜ਼ਦੀ ਮਨਜ਼ੂਰ ਗੁਰੁ ਗੋਬਿੰਦ ਸਿੰਘ॥
ਹੱਕ ਰਾ ਗੰਜੂਰ ਗੁਰੁ ਗੋਬਿੰਦ ਸਿੰਘ॥ ਜੁਮਲਾ ਫ਼ੈਜ਼ਿ ਨੂਰ ਗੁਰੁ ਗੋਬਿੰਦ ਸਿੰਘ॥
ਹੱਕ ਹੱਕ ਆਗਾਹ ਗੁਰੁ ਗੋਬਿੰਦ ਸਿੰਘ॥ ਸ਼ਾਹਿ ਸ਼ਾਹਨਸ਼ਾਹ ਗੁਰੁ ਗੋਬਿੰਦ ਸਿੰਘ॥
ਬਰ ਦੋ ਆਲਮ ਸ਼ਾਹ ਗੁਰੁ ਗੋਬਿੰਦ ਸਿੰਘ॥ ਖ਼ਸਮ ਰਾ ਜਾਂ ਕਾਹ ਗੁਰੁ ਗੋਬਿੰਦ ਸਿੰਘ॥

Guru Gobind Singh is the helper of others and he has the help of God.
The Guru is the treasurer of God and bestower of merciful gifts.
The Guru knows God well and is the Emperor of Emperor.
The Guru is the king of both worlds and the warrior
who gives life to enemies.

- Bhai Nand Lal

Depicts the life of Guru Gobind Singh in 19 stars

400th anniversary of Amritsar foundation day was celebrated by SGPC, Amritsar in 1977-78 and the oil painting on the life of Guru Gobind Singh depicted in nineteen stars was chosen as the best one. President, SGPC, Amritsar S. G S Tohra honoured Artist Trilok Singh with a "Siropa" and cash award. This oil painting was kept by the SGPC, Amritsar for printing.

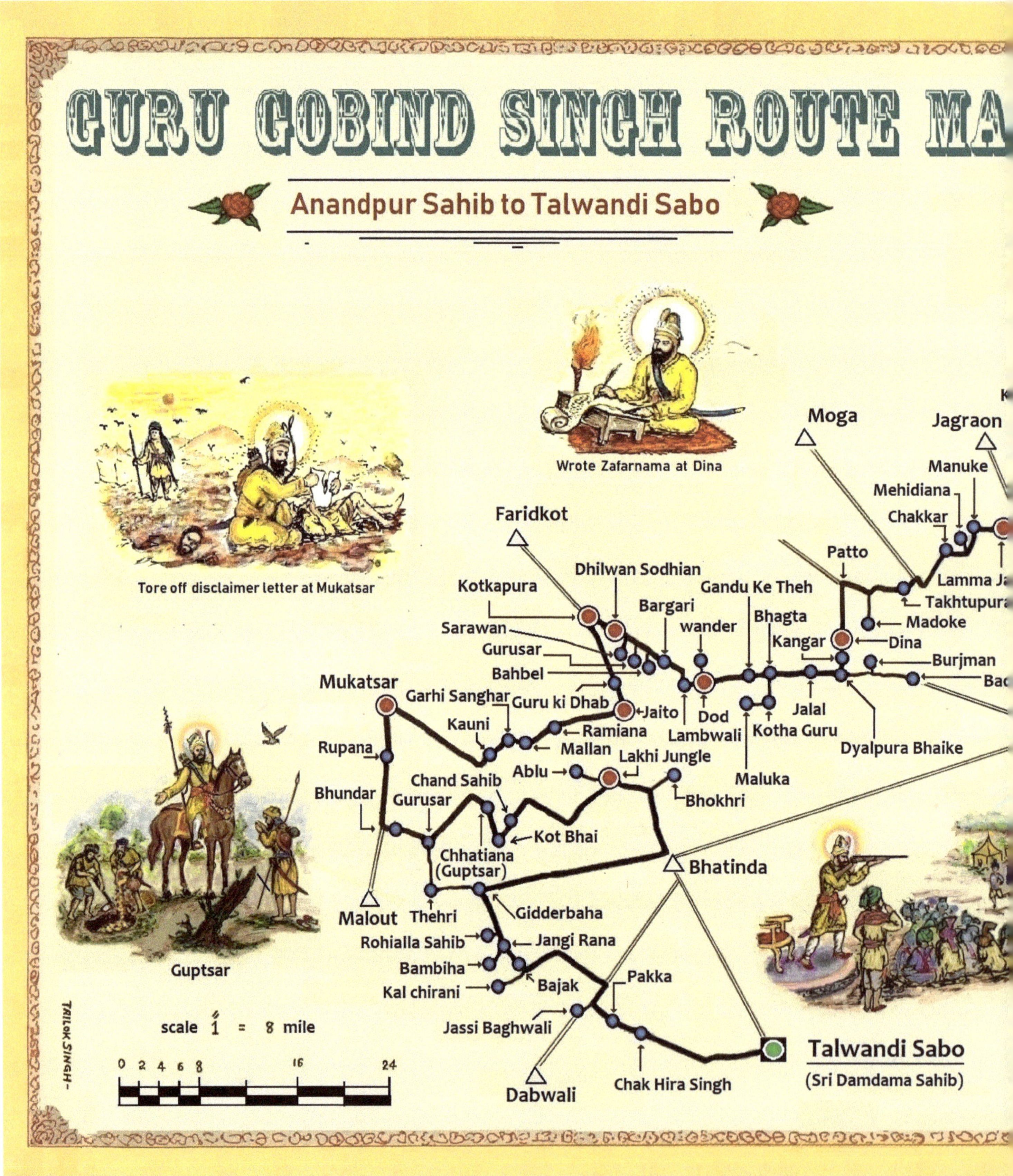

Guru Gobind Singh Marg - (Anandpur Sahib to Talwandi Sabo)

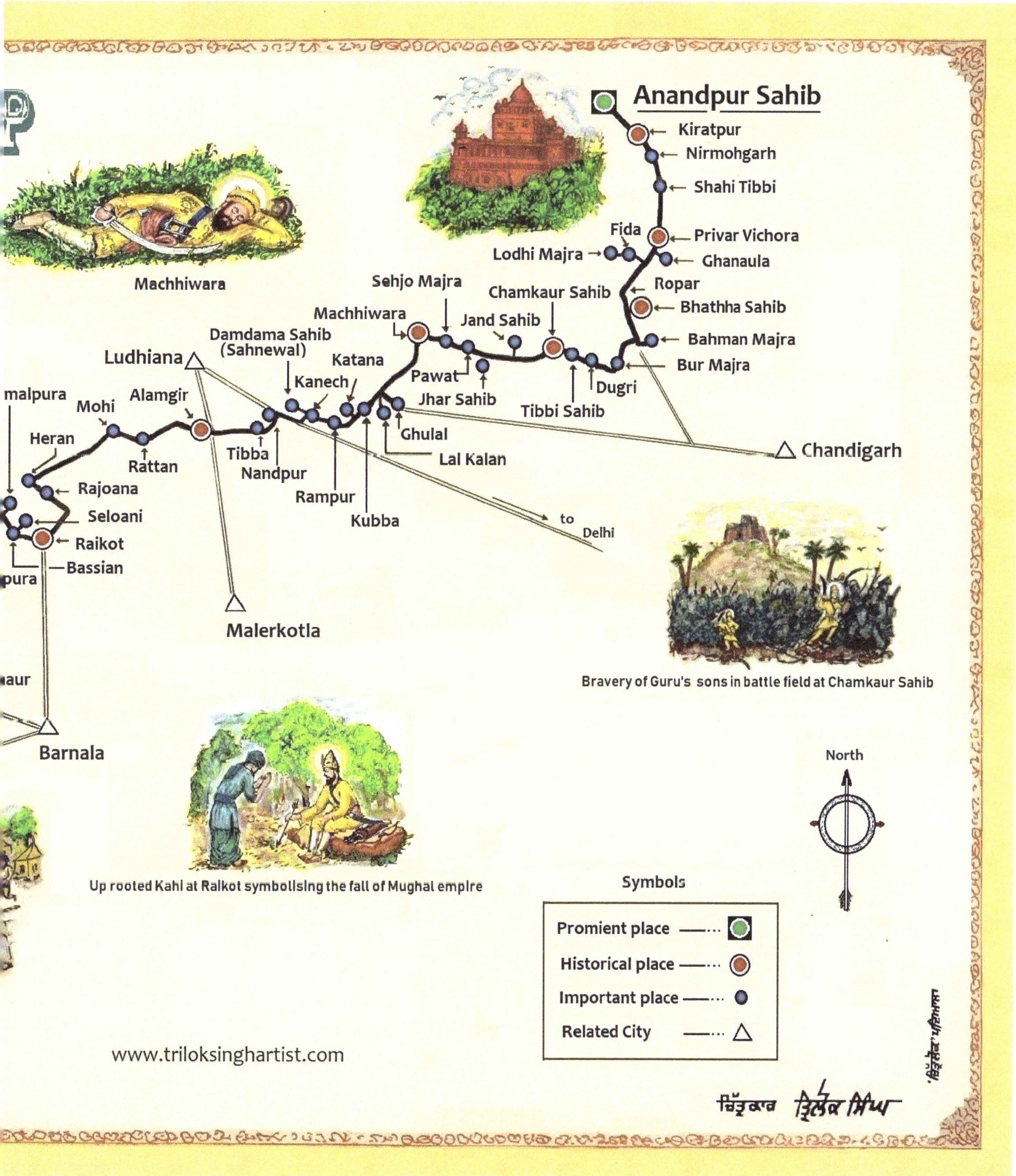

Anandpur Sahib
Kiratpur
Nirmohgarh
Shahi Tibbi
Fida
Privar Vichora
Lodhi Majra
Ghanaula
Machhiwara
Sehjo Majra
Ropar
Chamkaur Sahib
Bhathha Sahib
Machhiwara
Jand Sahib
Bahman Majra
Damdama Sahib (Sahnewal)
Ludhiana
Katana
Bur Majra
Pawat
Kanech
Dugri
malpura
Alamgir
Jhar Sahib
Mohi
Tibbi Sahib
Ghulal
Heran
Tibba
Lal Kalan
Chandigarh
Rattan
Nandpur
Rajoana
Rampur
Seloani
Kubba
to Delhi
Raikot
Bassian
pura
Malerkotla
aur
Bravery of Guru's sons in battle field at Chamkaur Sahib
Barnala
North
Up rooted Kahi at Raikot symbolising the fall of Mughal empire
Symbols
Promient place
Historical place
Important place
Related City
www.triloksinghartist.com
ਚਿੱਤ੍ਰਕਾਰ ਤ੍ਰਿਲੋਕ ਸਿੰਘ

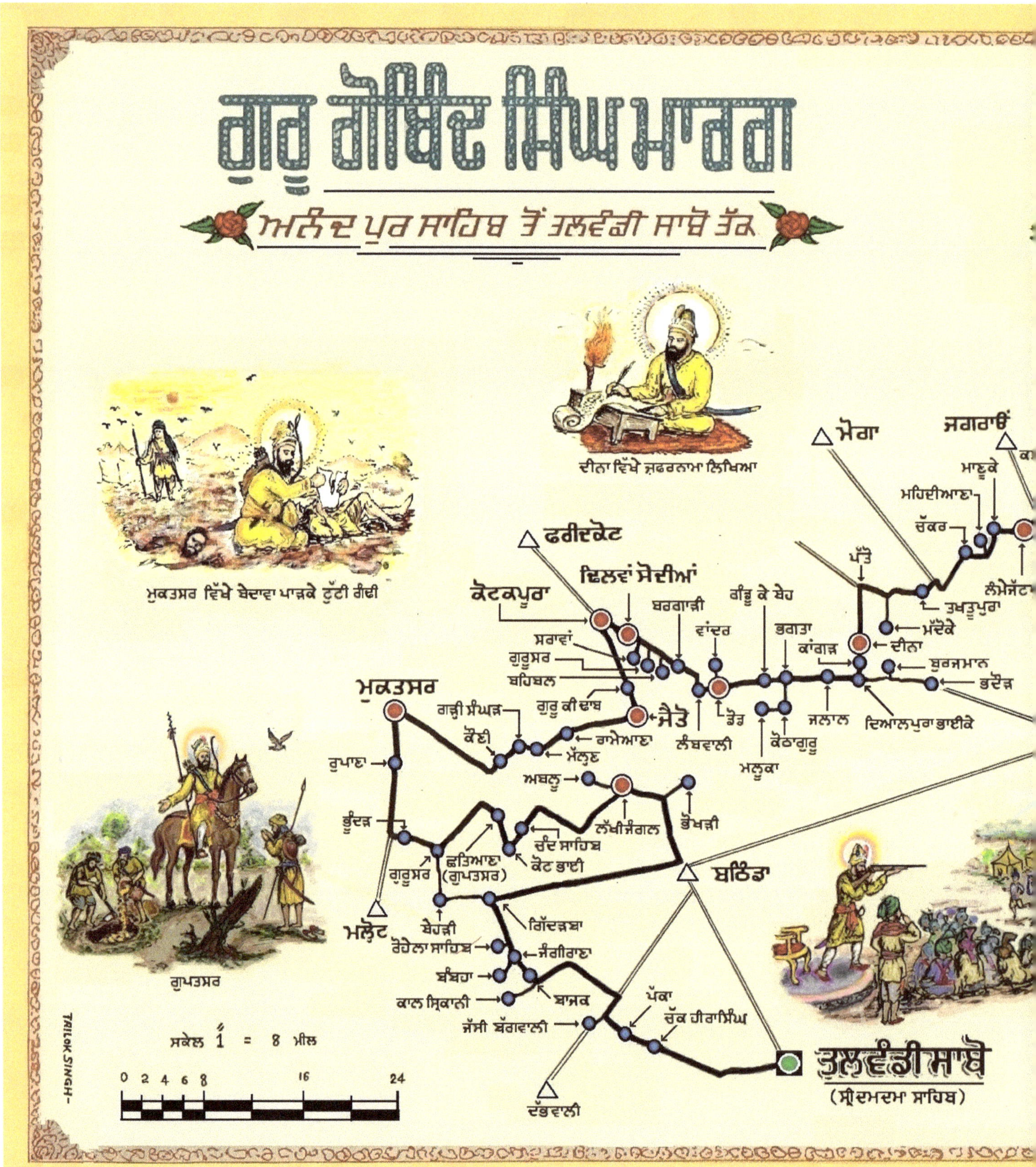

Guru Gobind Singh Marg -(Anandpur Sahib to Talwandi Sabo)

ਅਨੰਦ ਪੁਰ ਸਾਹਿਬ
ਕੀਰਤਪੁਰ
ਨਿਰਮੋਹਗੜ੍ਹ
ਸ਼ਾਹੀ ਟਿੱਬੀ
ਪਰਵਾਰ ਵਿਛੋੜਾ
ਘਨੌਲਾ
ਲੋਧੀ ਮਾਜਰਾ
ਰੋਪੜ
ਭੁੱਠਾ ਸਾਹਿਬ
ਚਮਕੌਰ ਸਾਹਿਬ
ਸਹਿਜੋ ਮਾਜਰਾ
ਜੰਡ ਸਾਹਿਬ
ਮਾਛੀਵਾੜਾ
ਬਾਹਮਣ ਮਾਜਰਾ
ਬੂਰ ਮਾਜਰਾ
ਦੁੱਘਰੀ
ਟਿੱਬੀ ਸਾਹਿਬ
ਤਾੜ ਸਾਹਿਬ
ਪਵਾਤ
ਲੁਧਿਆਣਾ
ਦਮਦਮਾ ਸਾਹਿਬ (ਸਾਹਨੇਵਾਲ)
ਕਟਾਣਾ
ਕਲੇਰ
ਘੁਲਾਲ
ਲੱਲਕਲਾਂ
ਕੁੱਬਾ
ਰਾਮਪੁਰ
ਨੰਦਪੁਰ
ਟਿੱਬਾ
ਆਲਮਗੀਰ
ਮੋਹੀ
ਰਤਨ
ਹੇਰਾਂ
ਰਾਜੋਆਣਾ
ਸੀਲੋਆਣੀ
ਰਾਏਕੋਟ
ਚੰਡੀਗੜ੍ਹ
ਦਿੱਲੀ ਨੂੰ
ਮਲੇਰਕੋਟਲਾ
ਬਰਨਾਲਾ
ਮਾਛੀਵਾੜਾ
ਚਮਕੌਰ ਸਾਹਿਬ ਦੀ ਜੰਗ ਵਿੱਚ ਸਾਹਿਬਜ਼ਾਦਿਆਂ ਦੀ ਬੀਰਤਾ
ਰਾਏਕੋਟ ਵਿੱਖੇ ਕਾਹੀ ਦੀ ਜੜ੍ਹ ਪੁੱਟਕੇ ਜ਼ੁਲਮੀ ਰਾਜ ਦੀ ਜੜ੍ਹ ਪੁੱਟੀ
ਸੰਕੇਤ :-
ਪ੍ਰਮੁੱਖ ਸਥਾਨ
ਇਤਿਹਾਸਕ ਸਥਾਨ
ਮਹਤਵ ਪੂਰਨ ਸਥਾਨ
ਸਮੀਪਤ ਨਗਰ
ਉੱਤਰ
www.triloksinghartist.com
ਭਾਸ਼ਾ ਵਿਭਾਗ, ਪੰਜਾਬ
ਚਿੱਤ੍ਰਕਾਰ ਤ੍ਰਿਲੋਕ ਸਿੰਘ

ਹੇ ਰਵਿ ਹੇ ਸਸਿ ਹੇ ਕਰੁਨਾਨਿਧਿ ਮੇਰੀ ਅਬੈ ਬਿਨਤੀ ਸੁਨ ਲੀਜੈ।
ਅਉਰ ਨਾ ਮਾਂਗਤ ਹਉ ਤੁਮ ਤੇ ਕਛੁ ਚਾਹਤ ਹਉ ਚਿਤ ਮੈ ਸੋਈ ਕੀਜੈ।
ਸਾਸਤ੍ਰਨ ਸੋ ਅਤਿ ਹੀ ਰਨ ਭੀਤਰ ਜੂਝ ਮਰੋ ਕਹਿ ਸਾਚ ਪਤੀਜੈ।
ਸੰਤ ਸਹਾਇ ਸਦਾ ਜਗ ਮਾਇ ਕ੍ਰਿਪਾ ਕਰ ਸਿਯਾਮ ਇਹੈ ਵਰੁ ਦੀਜੈ॥

The Guru prays to Almighty God, the creator of Sun and Moon to listen to his prayer. He prays to grant him his wish so that he may die in the battle field fighting courageously for the noble cause. Merciful God, Who takes care of His devotees and saints, may shower His grace on the Guru.

ANANDPUR SAHIB

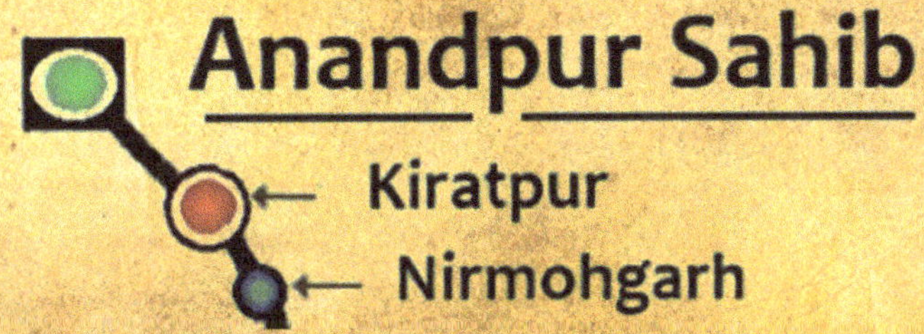

Anandpur Sahib means a city of bliss. It holds a very significant place in the history of world humanity. Guru Teg Bahadur (1621-1675 AD) bought land in Makhowal village and there founded the city and named it as 'Chak Nanaki' after his mother's name 'Nanaki'. A deputation of Kashmiri Pandits came to Anandpur Sahib to seek the help of the Guru against forcible conversion of religion. After nominating Gobind Rai as his successor, the Guru left for Delhi. Guru Teg Bahadur didn't accept Islam or perform miracle, thus attained martyrdom on November 11, 1675. Guru Gobind Singh was nine years old at that time.

Guru Gobind Singh received Bhai Jaita who had brought the beheaded head of Guru Teg Bahadur from Delhi. The Guru welcomed and embraced Bhai Jaita and said *Rangreta Guru Ka Beta*.

Guru Gobind Singh completed the work started by the first Guru - Guru Nanak Dev. He brought a revolution to abolish the various social evils present in the society.

After the victory of the imposed battle of Bhangani near Paonta Sahib by Hill-Rajas in 1685, Guru Gobind Singh shifted back to Anandpur Sahib. Later on, Anandpur Sahib became the center of Sikh activities. Guru Gobind Singh spent 30 years of his magnificent life journey at

Anandpur Sahib. Followers started getting training in weapons and horse riding. Many forts were constructed to safeguard Anandpur Sahib. A large number of Sikligars settled at Anandpur Sahib and manufactured swords and other weapons. During battles of Anandpur Sahib, Bhai Kanahiya started the service of looking after the wounded soldiers of both sides by providing them with water. The Guru appreciated his services and even gave ointment to apply on the wounds of the soldiers. Thus, the Guru preached and practised love for humanity and service for mankind. Later on, Red-cross society was founded on these principles.

The Guru abolished *Masand* system and asked the followers to come directly to Anandpur Sahib. People brought weapons and other gifts. Sikhs from Kabul gifted good horses, Raja Rattan Rai of Assam along with his mother came to Anandpur Sahib to meet the Guru and gifted a trained elephant named Parshadi Hathi, costly shamiana and other gifts. Horse traders started supplying best horses for the Sikhs warriors. The Guru continued the tradition of *Pangat and Sangat* as started by Guru Nanak.

Anandpur Sahib is the birth place of *Khalsa*. Guru Gobind Singh created *khalsa* - a community of saint-soldiers on the day of Baisakhi in 1699. On that day, the Guru gave authority to *Panj Pyare* (five beloved ones) to take decision in difficult times. The Guru got baptised by them. Thus, he became the Guru as well as the disciple.

The Guru prescribed certain code of conduct for truthful living. Khalsa has to maintain and keep Five *Ks* (comb, uncut hair, iron bracelet, sword and breeches). SINGH was added to the names of men and KAUR to women. Anandpur Sahib is one of the five *Takhats*, the most important religious place of Khalsa. By baptising the Sikhs, he infused such courage in ordinary people that they were ready to fight against the armed tyrant rulers. (*Sava Lakh Say Ek Ladaun*).

At Anandpur Sahib, the Guru started the tradition of Hola-Mahalla. The Sikhs were divided into two groups. They had to win the fort. In this mock fight, the winner team got appreciation by the Guru. The occasion was used to test the martial training of the Sikhs.

This all did not go well with high caste Hindus. The Hill-Rajas imposed many battles but could not succeed and then approached Mughal Emperor Aurangzeb to help them to oust the Guru and destroy Khalsa power. The combined forces of Hill-Rajas and Mughals attacked the Guru many times till 1704. The Khalsa army under the command of Guru Gobind Singh achieved victory every time. The combined forces under the command of Wazir Khan of Sarhind faced humiliating defeat every time.

The combined forces besieged Anandpur Sahib fort for about seven months in 1704. The combined forces took an oath on Quran, cow and Holy-book and requested the Guru to vacate Anandpur Sahib. On the solemn promise for a safe exit made by the enemy forces, the Guru's family members and Sikhs left Anandpur Sahib on 20th December 1704.

Guru Gobind Singh preached and practised democratic principles. *Panj Pyare* were given authority to give decision in difficult times. Every one had to bow before the decision. Even the Guru himself obeyed the decision taken by the *Panj Pyare*.

Gurdwara *Sri Keshgarh Sahib, Damaalgarh (Manji Sahib), Seesh Ganj, Akal Bunga, Guru ka Mahal, Damdama Sahib, Anand Garh, Lohgarh, Holegarh, Nirmohgarh* are the sacred places in Anandpur Sahib. These Gurdwaras keep the memories of the Saint-Soldier Guru Gobind Singh alive.

Guru Gobind Singh Marg starts from Anandpur Sahib.

ਜਉ ਕਿਛੁ ਇਛ ਕਰੋ ਧਨ ਕੀ ਤਉ ਚਲਿਯੋ ਧਨ ਦੇਸਨ ਦੇਸ ਤੇ ਆਵੈ।
ਅਉ ਸਬ ਰਿਧਨ ਸਿਧਨ ਪੈ ਹਮਰੋ ਨਹੀਂ ਨੈਕ ਜੀਯੰ ਲਲਚਾਵੇ।
ਅਉਰ ਸੁਨੋ ਕਛੁ ਜੋਗ ਬਿਖੈ ਕਹ ਕਉਨ ਇਤੇ ਤਪ ਕੈ ਤਨੁਤਾਵੈ।
ਜੂਝ ਮਰੋ ਰਨ ਮੈ ਤਜਿ ਭੈ ਤੁਮ ਤੈ ਪ੍ਰਭ ਸਯਾਮ ਇਹੈ ਵਰ ਪਾਵੈ।।

The Guru says that if he had wished for wealth, he could have collected
lot of money. He is not tempted for any miraculous powers.
He is not interested in realising God through physical austerities.
He prays to God to grant him His blessing to die fighting
courageously in the battle field for the noble cause.

Guru Teg Bahadur – 'Srishti di Chaddar'
ਗੁਰੂ ਤੇਗ ਬਹਾਦਰ - 'ਸ੍ਰਿਸ਼ਟੀ ਦੀ ਚਾਦਰ'

Guru Teg Bahadur (1621-1675) bought land in Makhowal village and founded a city, named it as 'Chak Nanaki' after his mother's name Nanaki. Now, it is known as Anandpur Sahib means city of bliss. A deputation of Kashmiri Pandits came to Anandpur Sahib to seek the help of Guru Teg Bahadur against forcible conversion of religion. After nominating Gobind Rai as his successor, the Guru left for Delhi. Guru Teg Bahadur didn't accept Islam or perform miracle, thus attained martyrdom on November 11, 1675.

In the painting, the Artist has shown the Guru sitting in a posture of a great saint on the platform of stones under a Banyan tree. Refusing to perform miracle or to accept Islam, the Guru chose the path of supreme sacrifice to save Hinduism and infuse courage and confidence in downtrodden people. He stood for freedom of faith. Thus, he is called 'Srishti Di Chaddar — ਸ੍ਰਿਸ਼ਟੀ ਦੀ ਚਾਦਰ।'

ਤੇਗ ਬਹਾਦਰ ਕੇ ਚਲਤ ਭਯੋ ਜਗਤ ਕੋ ਸੋਕ
ਹੈ ਹੈ ਹੈ ਸਭ ਜਗ ਭਯੋ ਜੈ ਜੈ ਜੈ ਸੁਰ ਲੋਕ।

After the martyrdom of Guru Teg Bahadur, Emperor Aurangzeb made sure that no body would take the body of the Guru and cremate it. Lakhi Shah Banjara, a local merchant, took the body of the Guru to his house and set the house on fire. On the other hand, Bhai Jaita took the beheaded head of the Guru reverently and started for Anandpur Sahib.

In the painting, the Artist has shown Bhai Jaita on the way to Anandpur Sahib carrying the head of the Guru with great respect and passing through thick forest. Fierce wind is blowing. Trees are showering their flowers on the Guru's head to welcome him to Heaven and branches in the sky formed the words 'Jai Jai Jai' means 'Jai Jai Jai Surlok – ਜੈ ਜੈ ਜੈ ਸੁਰ ਲੋਕ।' Similarly, the branches of a broken tree on earth form words 'Hai Hai Hai' means 'Hai Hai Hai Sab Jag Bhaio – ਹੈ ਹੈ ਹੈ ਸਭ ਜਗ ਭਯੋ।'

Guru Gobind Singh received Bhai Jaita who had brought the beheaded head of Guru Teg Bahadur to Anandpur Sahib. The Guru welcomed and embraced Bhai Jaita and said 'Rangreta Guru Ka Beta – ਰੰਘਰੇਟਾ ਗੁਰੂ ਕਾ ਬੇਟਾ।' He proved to be a true son.

Weapons are our Guru but Sikligars are their Gurus.
ਅਸਿ ਕ੍ਰਿਪਾਨ ਖੰਡੋ ਖੜਗ ਤੁਪਕ ਤਬਰ ਅਰੁ ਤੀਰ॥
ਸੈਫ ਸਰੋਹੀ ਸੈਹਥੀ ਯਹੈ ਹਮਾਰੇ ਪੀਰ॥

This historical painting illustrates Guru Gobind Singh's love and respect for various types of weapons. Sikligars were expert in making different kinds of weapons. Once the Guru sent some Nihang devotees to collect weapons from Sikligars. When they reached the spot they saw that the Sikligars were holding the weapons under their feet while grinding, polishing and giving final touches. They were furious to see this. They told the Sikligars that Guru Gobind Singh treated the weapons as His Guru and they were keeping the weapons under their feet. They should show some respect to the weapons. Sikligars tried to explain that this is the only way to give the final touch. But the Nihangs would not listen to this argument. So the Sikligars placed all the unfinished weapons in a big basket, covered the basket with a cloth and decorated it with flowers. They brought the basket and placed the unfinished weapons before the Guru. The Guru asked them the reason about the incomplete job done by them. They told the whole story to the Guru.

Then Guru Gobind Singh told the Nihang Sikhs that the weapons like sword, gun, spears, arrow, etc. are our gurus. We respect the weapons because they protect us from the tyrants, they are to be used for self defence and for protecting the weaker ones. But the Sikligars are the gurus of the weapons because they make them, grind them and polish them. Weapons are our guru but Sikligars are their gurus. As we salute the weapons, we should also salute their masters. They have to be given more respect than the weapons themselves.

This is the scene depicted in this painting. Sikligars have placed the weapons infront of the Guru. Guru Gobind Singh can be seen explaining about the respect to be shown to the weapon makers. His famous *Baaz* (falcon) is also shown. Fully armoured Nihangs are also shown in the picture.

On the right side, blacksmith's workshop has been shown. Fire is burning in furnace and air is pumped with bellow. A blacksmith is striking with a big hammer to give it proper shape. Some of the tampered and unpolished weapons are shown lying nearby.

On the leftside, Sikligars are holding the raw weapons with their feet for grinding, polishing and giving the final touch. At that time, Nihang Sikhs enter the workshop of Sikligars when they see all this, they are furious and argue with the Sikligars.

Different types of weapons have been shown in the painting i.e. Us (ਅਸਿ - sword), Kirpan (ਕ੍ਰਿਪਾਨ - a curved sword), Kharg (ਖੜਗ - Straight and heavy sword), Khando (ਖੰਡੋ – Double edged sword), Tubak (ਤੁਪਕ - Gun), Tabar (ਤਬਰ - similar to an axe as shown), teer (ਤੀਰ - arrows), Saif (ਸੈਫ਼ - straight sword), Saahthi (ਸੈਹਥੀ - spear). All the different kinds of weapons were used in battle in those days.

In Urdu, it is written Degh Tegh Fateh (ਦੇਗ ਤੇਗ ਫਤਿਹ) - means dual responsibility of Khalsa to provide food and protection to the needy and oppressed ones.

This was the last painting by the Artist.

ਸਾਸਤ੍ਰਨ ਸੋ ਅਤਿ ਹੀ ਰਨ ਭੀਤਰ ਜੂਝ ਮਰੋ ਕਹਿ ਸਾਚ ਪਤੀਜੈ।

The Guru says that if he falls a martyr while fighting courageously
for the noble cause then he thinks he has realised the Truth.

It is not the Sikh but his life and conduct that is dear to the Guru.
ਰਹਿਣੀ ਰਹੇ ਸੋਈ ਸਿੱਖ ਮੇਰਾ

The historical painting depicts Guru Gobind Singh's views on living a worthy life. He always believed in working hard and earning one's livelihood honestly. He always instilled in his disciples the importance of hard work. It is not the Sikh but his life and conduct that is dear to the Guru. Hands and feet that are not put to the service of others are worthless in the eyes of the Guru. There are many anecdotes illustrating this view.

The Artist has depicted one such anecdote in this painting. One day, the Guru asked for water. A rich Khatri boy sitting nearby brought a glass of water and offered it to the Guru. The Guru noticed that his hands were very delicate and soft. He asked the boy had he ever employed his hands in some sort of work. The boy replied that this is the first time that he had used them in any kind of work. Then the Guru refused to accept water from such hands. He believed in the dignity of labour. The body which is not used in the service of others is worthless. The life and conduct of a Sikh is dear to the Guru. From then onward, the boy vowed to lead his life according to the teachings of the Guru.

The Guru's room has been shown in the painting. His bow and arrow and lots of books are lying nearby. His famous *Baaz* (falcon) is also perched there.

On the top of the painting, the Artist has written that true Sikh is the one who leads a truthful life according to the teachings of the Guru. The body that is not put to the service of others is worthless.

ਇਨ ਹੀ ਕੀ ਕ੍ਰਿਪਾ ਕੇ ਸਜੇ ਹਮ ਹੈ ਨਹੀਂ ਮੋ ਸੇ ਗਰੀਬ ਕਰੋਰ ਪਰੇ।

The Guru says that he has been elevated by the grace of Almighty God, otherwise there are millions of poor people like him.

'It is by practice but not magical power' — Guru Gobind Singh —
'ਕਰਾਮਾਤ ਨਹੀਂ ਕਰਤੱਬ ਹੈ'

This historical painting depicts the scene at Anandpur Sahib. Combined forces of Hill-Rajas and Mughals had besieged the Anandpur fort. The battle continued for a long time. In the painting, the Artist has shown Guru Gobind Singh with bow and arrow. The Guru sent an arrow to the enemy camp at a distance of about three miles. The enemy thought that it is due to some magical powers. Then, the Guru shot another arrow along with a written message 'It is by practice, not magical power.' The Gurus never believed in performing miracles. They believed in laying down their lives for a noble cause than saving themselves by performing miracles. The Guru in the painting is shown fully armoured. Nagara (ਨਗਾਰਾ) is also lying there. Guru's bows, arrows, paper, ink pot and feather used to write, are also shown in the painting. Some other armoured Sikhs are also shown behind the Guru.

PRIVAR VICHORA

Guru Gobind Singh with family members and about five hundred Sikhs left Anandpur Sahib at the dead of the night on December 20, 1704. The mid winter night was dark, cold and windy. It was raining heavily.

When the combined forces of Hill-Rajas and Mughals realised that the Guru and Sikhs have gone during the night, they lost no time in getting ready to chase and attack them. They forgot all about the oaths taken on Quran, cow and Holy-book for the safe passage for vacating the town of Anandpur Sahib. But the Guru did not lose faith in the Almighty and accepted His Will cheerfully.

After crossing Kiratpur, Nirmohgarh, the Guru along with Sikhs reached near Shahi Tibbi. Forces of Ajmer Chand, Hill-Raja of Kehlur attacked them. The Guru gave the responsibility to Bhai Udey Singh S/o Bhai Mani Singh along with 50 Sikhs to restrict the attack. A fierce battle took place, Bhai Udey Singh stopped the attack of the Hill-Rajas forces on the Sikhs crossing Shahi Tibbi but Bhai Udey Singh and many Sikhs achieved martyrdom. The Guru and other Sikhs proceeded ahead towards Ropar.

The Guru reached the bank of river Sirsa early in the morning and came to know that the combined forces of Hill-Rajas and Mughals were chasing them. The Guru gave responsibility to Bhai Jiwan Singh and 100 Sikhs to restrict the movement of attacking forces. Forces of Hill-Raja Ajmer Chand also reached river Sirsa from Shahi Tibbi and combined forces also started gathering there. Bhai Jiwan Singh and his team of Sikhs restricted the movement of combined forces for about six hours. Severe fighting took place, many brave Sikhs were killed.

The Guru halted on the bank of river Sirsa and recited morning prayer *'Asa Di Var'* peacefully. The river was in flood. After the prayers, preparations were made to cross the river. *Sahibzada* Ajit Singh with number of Sikhs valiantly arrested the progress of the enemy so that the Guru and others could cross the river. Later on, they joined the Guru on the other side of the river.

In this confusion, the Guru's mother Mata Gujri and two younger *Sahibzadas* Zorawar Singh and Fateh Singh got separated from the main group. Mata Sundri and Mata Sahib Kaur proceeded to Delhi with Bhai Mani Singh and few Sikhs. The Guru, his two elder sons along with Sikhs including five *Pyare* started towards Ropar.

Gurdwara *Privar Vichora* exists where the Guru's family got separated from the main party of the Sikhs. It is built on a hill top and gives a panoramic view.

ਹਮਰੀ ਕਰੋ ਹਾਥ ਦੈ ਰੱਛਾ॥ ਪੂਰਨ ਹੋਇ ਚਿੱਤ ਕੀ ਇੱਛਾ॥
ਤਵ ਚਰਨਨ ਮਨ ਰਹੈ ਹਮਾਰਾ॥ ਅਪਨਾ ਜਾਨ ਕਰੋ ਪ੍ਰਤਿਪਾਰਾ॥

The Guru prays to Almighty God to always keep His protective hand on his head.
May all our desires be fulfilled and our mind may always be fixed
on God's feet. May the God nurture us as His sons.

Mata Gujri with younger Sahibzadas

While crossing river Sirsa, Mata Gujri with her two younger grandsons got separated from the main group. Later on they met Gangu Brahmin, who was a cook at Anandpur Sahib. He promised to take them to a safe place and give them shelter and protection in his house in village Seheri on Ropar-Morinda road.

In this painting, the Artist has shown Mata Gujri with her two younger grandsons in her lap covered with a blanket and sitting on a pony. A money bag is also shown loaded on the pony. Gangu Brahmin is taking them to his house. The facial expression of Gangu Brahmin shows that he is planning something different for them. He is lured by the wealth and plans to give them away to the Governor of Sarhind, Wazir Khan.

The Artist has beautifully shown in the painting that coming events cast their shadows before. A dark cloud takes the shape of a crocodile with mouth open to catch flying swans. A vulture shown sitting on a dry tree waiting for a dead animal is also a sign of something bad to happen. The scenic beauty is par excellence and is of Ropar area.

Mata Gujri with younger Sahibzadas

ਧੰਨ ਜੀਉ ਤਿਹ ਕੋ ਜਗ ਮੈ ਮੁਖ ਤੇ ਹਰਿ ਚਿੱਤ ਮੈਂ ਜੁਧੁ ਬਿਚਾਰੈ।

Bravo the soul of that person who remembers the Almighty God & reflects in his mind about the war of righteousness.

BHATHHA SAHIB

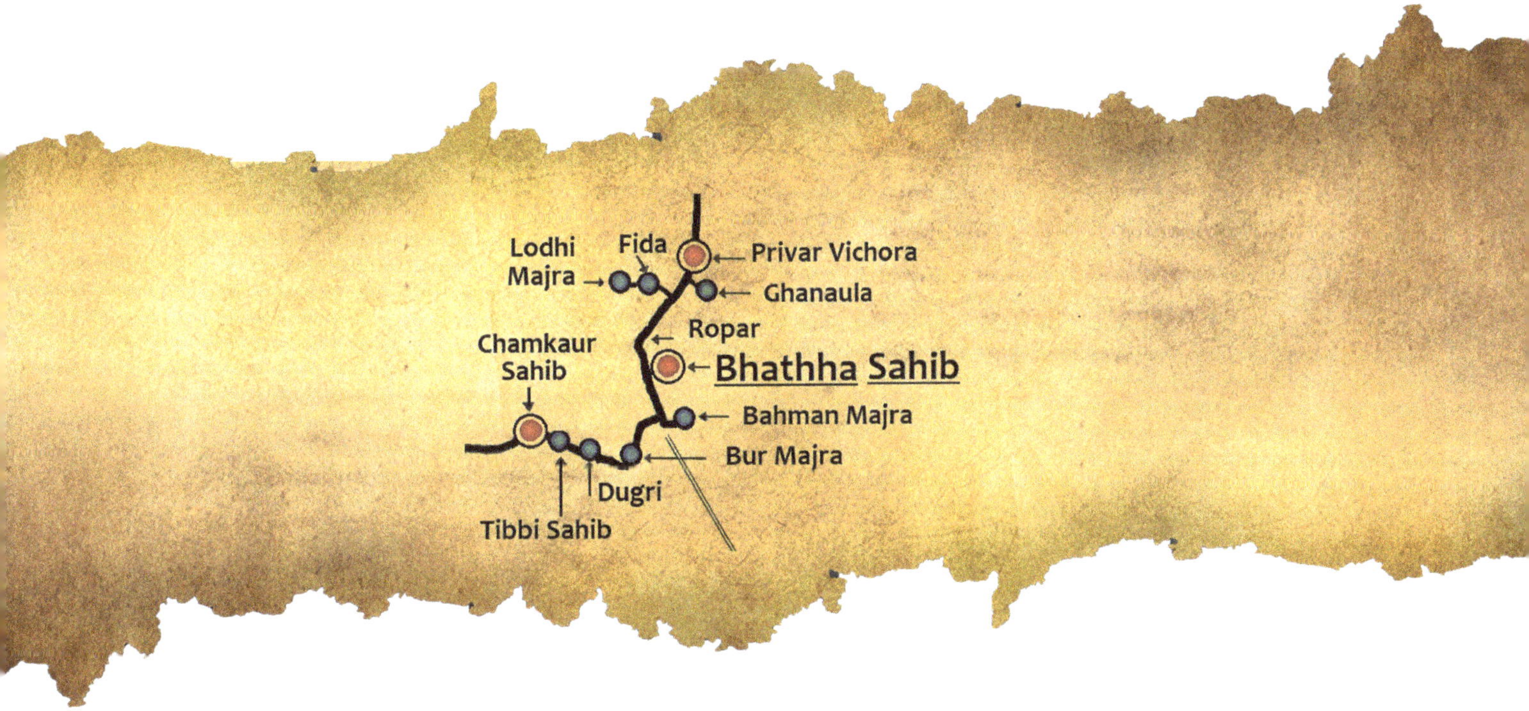

After crossing river Sirsa, Guru Gobind Singh with Sikhs proceeded towards Ropar. They reached Ghanauli, but the route ahead was not safe. Pathans and Ranghars came to know about the Sikhs coming towards Ropar. The Guru ordered Bhai Bachittar Singh and about 100 Sikhs to reach Kotla Nihang Khan at Ropar via Malikpur. On the way to Ropar, Muslim Rangars stopped the Sikhs at Malikpur and attacked them. A fierce battle took place. They defeated the Muslim Rangars in the battle and proceeded ahead. Many brave Sikhs achieved martyrdom while fighting with them. Bhai Bachittar Singh was wounded severely in the battle. He was taken to the Haveli of Nihang Khan. The Guru and other Sikhs reached the Haveli of Nihang Khan via Fida. Nihang Khan, without bothering about any danger to him, opened the doors of his Haveli and welcomed the Guru and Sikhs and helped them with full devotion.

The Guru stayed in the Haveli of Nihang Khan (presently, known as Bhathha Sahib) for some time. A follower devotee informed the Guru that the combined forces of Hill-Rajas and Mughals were chasing them. The condition of Bhai Bachittar Singh (son of Bhai Mani Singh) became serious. The Guru left Bhai Bachittar Singh in the care of Nihang Khan.

The Guru with two elder Sahibzadas and Sikhs proceeded towards Chamkaur Sahib hurriedly. The Mughal forces chasing the Guru reached the Haveli of Nihang Khan and did a thorough search. Nihang Khan told the soldiers that his daughter and son-in-law were in the room. The soldiers left. The daughter heard her father's words, and she did not marry afterward and told her father that she had accepted his words. Bhai Bachittar Singh died, later on, due to wounds.

The Guru blessed Nihang Khan happily with:

1. The Sri Sahib (This sword was presented to the Guru by the Royal family of Ghazni through Bhai Nand Lal, a Persian scholar. On the backside of the sword 'Shahin Shah Muhmood Mamoor' was inscribed.)
2. The Shield (*Dhal*)
3. The Katar Sahib.

In 1947, before Nihang Khan's family left for Pakistan, they handed over the Guru's weapons to the historical Gurdwara Bhathha Sahib, Village Kotla Nihang Khan, Ropar. The Guru's weapons are displayed there.

Guru Gobind Singh had visited this place thrice before.

Firstly, when the Guru was returning to Anandpur Sahib after winning the battle of Bhangani in 1686. He asked for a place to stay, the labourer working at the *Bhathha* (brick kiln) pointed towards the burning kiln. As soon as Guru's horse stepped on the kiln, the burning kiln became cold. Frightened, the labourer ran and told the owner of the kiln, Nihang Khan, the local chief. He was a true devotee of the Guru and used to supply horses to the Guru. He instantly rushed to the *Bhathha* and saw the Guru sitting there. He bowed his head reverently and asked for forgiveness. He took the Guru to his fort.

Secondly, the Guru came to attend the engagement ceremony of Nihang Khan's son.

Thirdly, when he was returning from Kurukshetra.

ਸਗਲ ਦੁਆਰ ਕੋ ਛਾਡਿ ਕੈ ਗਹਿਓ ਤੁਹਾਰੋ ਦੁਆਰ ॥
ਬਾਹਿ ਗਹੇ ਕੀ ਲਾਜਿ ਅਸ ਗੋਬਿੰਦ ਦਾਸ ਤੁਹਾਰ ॥

The Guru says that he has completely and unconditionally surrendered himself to the Lord's Will. He is at the mercy of God. Now, it is for the God to protect him as he is God's servant.

Guru Gobind Singh came to spread dharma, protect saints and root out tyrants.

This historic painting by Trilok Singh (1914-90) depicts that Guru Gobind Singh came to spread dharma, protect saints and root out tyrants and evil-minded persons. (ਧਰਮ ਚਲਾਵਨ ਸੰਤ ਉਬਾਰਨ। ਦੁਸਟ ਸਭਨ ਕੋ ਮੂਲ ਉਪਾਰਨ।।)

Guru Gobind Singh has been shown coming into this world to spread the message of love, truthfulness, courage, bravery, and willpower to live and die for the noble ideals.

Guru Gobind Singh has a string of beads (Mala) in one hand and a sword in the other hand indicating that one must lead a spiritual life as well as be prepared to defend himself and the weaker sections of the society.

All the religions are the ways to reach out to the Lord Almighty. Religions are different roads leading to the same destination. Sikhism is a way of life. Throughout their lives, the Gurus practised what they preached. They led the householder's life and remained detached from worldly attractions.

The Guru, himself has written in the Bachitar Natak that he had been ordered and sent by the Supreme God to witness the drama of life. (ਮੈ ਹੋ ਪਰਮ ਪੁਰਖ ਕੋ ਦਾਸਾ। ਦੇਖਨਿ ਆਯੋ ਜਗਤ ਤਮਾਸਾ।।)

He came into this world to accomplish the task started by the first Guru, Guru Nanak Dev. The social, moral and religious values were at the lowest ebb when Guru Nanak came into this world. He laid the foundation of a new kind of religion which would enable the people to stand erect and united against the oppressors and also to lead a householder's life. They will live in this world but remain detached from the worldly attractions as a lotus grows in muddy water and remains unaffected by the dirt around it. All the Gurus carried forward these ideals of Guru Nanak.

When Guru Gobind Singh came into this world, the Mughal Empire was at its zenith, so were the atrocities of the Mughal rulers. Guru Gobind Singh created Khalsa - an army of saint soldiers. They were always ready to lay down their lives for a good cause. The Guru always prayed to God Almighty that he would die in the battle-field fighting for a good cause.

'The world is afraid of death - that death fills my mind with bliss. It is only by death that perfect supreme bliss is obtained.' (ਜਿਸੁ ਮਰਨੇ ਤੇ ਜਗੁ ਡਰੈ ਮੇਰੈ ਮਨਿ ਆਨੰਦੁ) Death fills my mind with bliss. Supreme bliss is achieved through death. Here the Guru is not referring to the physical death of the person but the death of five vices present in human beings. Sex, Anger, Greed, Love, and Ego (ਕਾਮ, ਕ੍ਰੋਧ, ਲੋਭ, ਮੋਹ, ਹੰਕਾਰ) are worldly vices that lead the person away from the spiritual path. All the Gurus stressed that a person should control these vices and win over them. They should live the life of a householder and still remain detached from these worldly attractions. As a lotus grows in muddy water and still keeps the dirt away, similarly a person has to live in this world and control the vices. When he has killed these vices, only then he can have the feeling of supreme bliss.

The Artist has shown the globe and a learned old man, at the fag end of his life. He is afraid to face death. Hammer of death is about to strike him. He has closed his eyes as he does not have the courage to face death. This is the reality. Everyone, rich or poor, religious or non-believer is afraid of death.

In the painting, a ship has been shown sailing in turbulent waters. A shark is making its journey difficult. Some people are about to drown and are crying for help. The rough sea is symbolic of the difficulties of life. A man has to face many ups and downs in his life. The women were always in danger. The people are also afraid to take challenges. Only God's name can alleviate the sufferings and can help to cross the ocean of worldly attractions.

Death (ਮੌਤ ਰਾਣੀ) has always been believed to have an ugly-looking face. The Artist, in the light emanating from Guru Gobind Singh's sword, has shown the death queen is not an ugly-looking one but a very beautiful lady, and the brave men are going to meet her smilingly. One should not be afraid of death but should be ready to face it courageously.

Guru Gobind Singh created Khalsa which would work for the upliftment of the downtrodden masses and help them to lead a truthful and righteous life. Fear not and frighten not will be their motto. And ready to fight for noble cause and achieve victory with determination.

ਜੋ ਹਮ ਕੋ ਪਰਮੇਸਰ ਉਚਰਿ ਹੈ ਤੈ ਸਭ ਨਰਕ ਕੁੰਡ ਮਹਿ ਪਰਿ ਹੈ।
ਮੋ ਕੋ ਦਾਸ ਤਵਨੁ ਕਾ ਜਾਨੋ ਯਾ ਮੈ ਭੇਦ ਨ ਰੰਚ ਪਛਾਨੋ।
ਮੈ ਹੋ ਪਰਮ ਪੁਰਖ ਕੋ ਦਾਸਾ ਦੇਖਨਿ ਆਯੋ ਜਗਤ ਤਮਾਸਾ॥

All those who call me God shall fall into Hell. Consider me as mere servant of God, there is no doubt in it. I am the servant of Supreme Lord and have come to witness the drama of life.

CHAMKAUR SAHIB

Sufi Shayar Alha Yaar Khan wrote that Chamkaur Sahib is the only sacred place of pilgrimage in India to be visited, where the Guru sacrificed his sons in the name of Almighty.

"ਬਸ ਏਕ ਹਿੰਦ ਮੇ ਤੀਰਥ ਹੈ, ਯਾਤਰਾ ਕੇ ਲਿਯੇ।
ਕਟਾਏ ਬਾਪ ਨੇ ਬੱਚੇ ਜਹਾਂ, ਖੁਦਾ ਕੇ ਲਯੇ। ।"

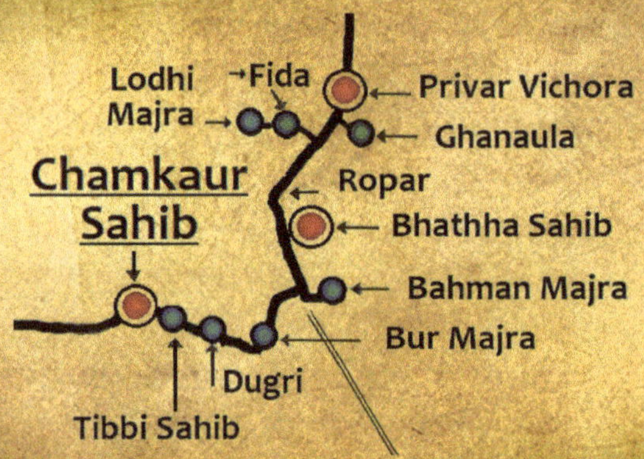

Guru Gobind Singh, with his two elder sons and forty Sikhs, left the Haveli of Nihang Khan, hurriedly. On reaching Bur Majra, the Guru got the news that combined forces were chasing them. The Guru knew the area of Chamkaur Sahib. On reaching there, the Guru selected a mud-built Haveli on the mound top from battle point of view. They had limited number of arms. The Sikhs were famished and tired but had undaunted courage, determination, willpower and belief in God Almighty. It was evening time. They occupied a mud-built Haveli on a hilltop, offered by a devotee. Sikhs took their position for battle there. Ten lakh combined forces of Hill-Rajas and Mughals reached Chamkaur Sahib and surrounded the Haveli. Commander of the combined forces, Nawab Wazir Khan's offer to spare them if they come out of the Haveli, was rejected by Guru Gobind Singh. The Guru and Sikhs became ready for the battle. One group of the forces led by Mughal General Nahar Khan started climbing up the wall of the mud-built Haveli. Nahar Khan was shot down by the Guru's arrow, and others fell back.

On December 22, 1704, there began one of the most heroic and unique battles. It has no parallel in the annals of human history. Forty famished Sikhs on one side and ten lakh combined forces of Hill-Rajas and Mughals with unlimited supplies, on the other hand, circled around them. Here the Guru proved the truth of his saying that he would cause the sparrows to fight with the hawks. (ਚਿੜੀਓ ਸੇ ਮੈਂ ਬਾਜ ਲੜਾਉ ਤਬੈ ਗੋਬਿੰਦ ਸਿੰਘ ਨਾਮ ਕਹਾਉ।।)

The combined forces surrounded the old mud Haveli and wanted to attack in one attempt. Sikhs went out to fight in batches of five each, roaring the *Jaikara 'Bolle So Nihal Sat Sri Akal'. It* echoed throughout the battlefield. They fought bravely, killing a large number of enemy soldiers. Guru Gobind Singh was watching the battle scene from the top of the Haveli and rained volley of arrows on enemy soldiers to provide protection to the Sikhs fighting in the battlefield. Sahibzada Ajit Singh requested the Guru to send him out to fight along with the Sikhs.

Nowhere in the whole history, there exists an example where the father himself has sent out his son to sure death. He prepared his son, embraced and blessed him for the last time. Ajit Singh fought like a lion killing a large number of soldiers. The father Guru had been watching his son from the top storey, admiring and rejoicing at his son's marvellous bravery. When he fell down while fighting, the Guru thanked the God Almighty. Then, the second son of the Guru, Shahibzada Jujhar Singh came and asked for permission to go out in the battlefield. The Guru embraced, blessed and patted him and gave him a sword and a shield. He also fought valiantly, but before falling down, he killed many soldiers. All odds were against him. In the end, he was overpowered and died fighting bravely. Guru thanked the God that his sons have proved worthy of his noble cause.

When the battle was stopped for the night, the remaining Sikhs thought for the sake of *Khalsa*, the Guru had to go out to a safer place. If the Guru is safe, he can raise more saint-soldiers like us. Five Sikhs passed a *Gurmata* (resolution) and commanded the Guru to leave Chamkaur Sahib. The Guru had to bow before the *Gurmata.* It was decided that Bhai Daya Singh, Dharam Singh, and Man Singh would accompany the Guru. Bhai Sangat Singh and the remaining Sikhs would remain there to fight the enemy so that the Guru could move away. The Guru and his three companions left the Haveli in different directions. At some distance, the Guru clapped three times and exclaimed "*Pir-e-Hind Mey Rawad* (The Guru is going - ਪੀਰੇ ਹਿੰਦ ਮੇ ਰਵੱਦ)" means the Guru of the Sikhs is going.

Bhai Sangat Singh, whose built and face resembled the Guru, was made to wear the Guru's plume. He occupied Guru's place on the top of the Haveli and the remaining Sikhs stationed themselves in the top storey. The next day, they resisted the attack of the combined forces valiantly and died a heroic death after killing a number of enemy soldiers with arrows. When the Mughals saw the handsome slim body of Sangat Singh, they mistook him as the Guru and their joy knew no bounds.

There are many Gurdwaras in Chamkaur Sahib to commemorate the visit of the Guru, the martyrdom of the Sahibzadas and the brave Sikhs. Gurdwara *Qatalgarh Sahib, Garhi Sahib, Taari Sahib, Ranjit Garh, Damdama Sahib* are some of the famous historical Gurdwaras.

Guru Gobind Singh blessing his son to fight for the right and noble cause.

The historical painting by the Artist depicts the greatest acts of courage of Guru Gobind Singh and sacrifice in the annals of history. The Artist has shown no pain or regret on Guru's face, only happiness and admiration for his son's courage while sending his sons to sure death.

The Guru has written his wish 'ਸਸਤ੍ਰਨ ਸੋਂ ਅਤਿ ਹੀ ਰਨ ਭੀਤਰ ਜੂਝ ਮਰੋਂ ਕਹਿ ਸਾਚ ਪਤੀਜੈ।' The Guru wished that if he dies a martyr while fighting for a noble cause then he would think that he has realised the truth.

This kind of courage, bravery, and spirit to fight for the right and noble cause has no parallel in the history. Guru Gobind Singh has written '... ਜੂਝ ਮਰਹੁੰ ਰਨ ਮੈ ਤਜਿ ਭੈ ...।'

The Guru with his two sons and forty tired and famished Sikhs faced ten lakh combined forces of the Hill-Rajas and Mughals at Chamkaur Sahib. The combined forces were certain that they will certainly kill or capture the Guru along with his Sikhs in a few hours. Sikhs fought valiantly and courageously under the planned strategy with the large enemy forces from morning till nightfall.

The Guru knew what the end of his sons would be. The Guru not only gave them permission to go out and fight with the enemy but also gave them bows, arrows, sword and shield. He embraced and blessed his elder son Ajit Singh for the last time and sent him unto a certain death. Then he permitted his second son Jujhar Singh.

Sufi Shayar Alha Yaar Khan wrote about the courage of the Guru at the time of Chamkaur Sahib battle:-

"ਲੇ ਜਾਓ ਸਿਧਾਰੋ, ਤੁਮ੍ਹੇ ਕਰਤਾਰ ਕੋ ਸੋਂਪਾ।
ਮਰ ਜਾਓ ਯਾ ਮਾਰੋ, ਤੁਮ੍ਹੇ ਕਰਤਾਰ ਕੋ ਸੋਂਪਾ।
ਰੱਬ ਕੋ ਨਾ ਬਿਸਾਰੋ, ਤੁਮ੍ਹੇ ਕਰਤਾਰ ਕੋ ਸੋਂਪਾ।
ਵਾਹਗੁਰੂ ਅਬ ਜੰਗ ਕੀ ਹਿੰਮਤ ਤੁਮ੍ਹੇ ਬਖਸ਼ੇ।
ਪਿਆਸੇ ਹੋ ਜਾਤੇ, ਜਾਮਿ ਸ਼ਹਾਦਤ ਤੁਮ੍ਹੇ ਬਖਸ਼ੇ।"

The Artist prepared this beautiful painting in 1976.

First Sikh woman martyr Bibi Sharan Kaur at Chamkaur Sahib

First Sikh woman martyr Bibi Sharan Kaur. She was a very brave and courageous lady, she collected the bodies of Sahibzada Ajit Singh, Jujhar Singh, and of many other Sikh martyrs. She also brought the wood. Then she lit the pyre. When the Mughals saw the fire, they came there and saw Bibi Sharan Kaur cremating the bodies. To save her honour, she jumped into the funeral pyre. This way the brave fearless woman attained martyrdom. She is the first Sikh woman to attain this feat.

The Artist has beautifully illustrated this scene in the painting.

ਪਾਹਿ ਗਹੇ ਜਬ ਤੇ ਤੁਮਰੇ ਤਬ ਤੇ ਕੋਊ ਅਖਿ ਤਰੈ ਨਹੀਂ ਆਨਿਓ।

After the Guru took refuge at Almighty God's feet, he has never looked for protection from any other.

MACHHIWARA

After accepting *Gurmata* (Resolution) of five Sikhs, the Guru along with three Sikhs, Bhai Daya Singh, Bhai Dharam Singh, and Bhai Man Singh moved out of the Chamkaur Haveli separately in the night. Instead of leaving the Haveli silently, Guru clapped three times at some distance and exclaimed "*Pir-e-Hind Mey Rawad*" that the Guru is going.

For days, the Guru and the Sikhs had been without food or proper rest. The Guru reached the outskirts of Machhiwara - a desolate place and forest after passing through various villages, Jand, Jhar, Pawat, Sehjomajra. The Guru's bare feet got wounded due to long walking. Tired, the Guru lay down in the cluster of trees, his hands clasped the sword, he fell asleep. Here he composed his famous hymn "*Mitre Pyare noon, Haal Muridan da Kehna...*"

This garden belonged to a *Masand* named Gulaba. Bhai Dharam Singh, Daya Singh, and Man Singh reached there while searching for the Guru. They woke him up. The Guru could not move because of cuts/ blisters on his feet. Bhai Man Singh carried him on his back to a well in the garden. There the Guru bathed and felt refreshed. Amidst all these difficulties and tough situations, the Guru thanked God Almighty.

Gulaba also came there and met the Guru. He served milk and food to the Guru and the Sikhs. All rested in the garden while Gulaba guarded the garden. At night, they took the Guru to a room in the upper storey of Gulaba's house. Now Gurdwara *Chaubara Sahib* exists there. The next day, Gulaba put up the fear of the chasing Mughal forces and requested the Guru to move to a safe place. The Guru keeping in view this situation prepared to move.

Gani Khan and Nabi Khan, two Rohilla Pathans of Machhiwara, used to supply horses to the Guru at Anandpur Sahib. They also heard about the Guru, met him and took him to their house respectfully. There, they planned to dress the Guru as '*Uch Da Pir*'. Hardeyi, an old lady living there had woven a cloth for the Guru and planned to present it to him. Gani Khan and Nabi Khan told Hardeyi that the time has come to present the cloth to the Guru for preparing the dress. They took the cloth from her, dyed it blue, and stitched a robe for the Guru. They did it very cautiously as combined forces were all around there. Thus, they disguised the Guru as *Uch Da Pir*. Gani Khan, Nabi Khan, Bhai Man Singh, Daya Singh, and Dharam Singh carried the Guru in a specially prepared *Manji* (palanquin). Four of them carried the palanquin on their shoulders and the fifth one doing Chaur Sahib. Whoever questioned them on the way, was told that they were taking *Uch Da Pir*.

When they were moving out of Machhiwara, Mughal forces stationed there, stopped them. Their commander Dilawar Khan wanted to check the identity of *Uch Da Pir*. As a test, he asked them to share a meal with the Muslims. He knew that the Sikhs would not share a meal with the Muslims. The *Pir* asked his companions to eat after offering the food to the holy *Kirpan*. When his doubts were put to rest, the search party allowed them to carry on the journey. *Kirpan Bhent* Gurdwara is situated there.

ਚੱਤ੍ਰ ਚੱਕ੍ਰ ਵਰਤੀ ਚੱਤ੍ਰ ਚੱਕ ਭੁਗਤੇ ॥ ਸੁਯੰਭਵ ਸੁਭੰ ਸਰਬਦਾ ਸਰਬ ਜੁਗਤੇ ॥
ਦੁਕਾਲੰ ਪ੍ਰਣਾਸੀ ਦਿਆਲੰ ਸਰੂਪੇ ॥ ਸਦਾ ਅੰਗ ਸੰਗੇ ਅਭੰਗੰ ਬਿਭੂਤੇ ॥

The Guru says that God is present everywhere, in all directions and is the Creator as well as the Sustainer. The God self created, immanent, eternal and is the personification of mercy. Protects us all the time. He is always on our side.

Guru Gobind Singh in the forest of Machhiwara

ਮਿਤ੍ਰ ਪਿਆਰੇ ਨੂੰ ਹਾਲ ਮੁਰੀਦਾਂ ਦਾ ਕਹਿਣਾ

This is the scene, the Artist has depicted beautifully in this beautiful painting.

Here the Guru has been shown lying on the bed of grass, the left arm is folded and used as a pillow with the support of the shield and is taking rest. The Guru's face is a picture of spiritual glow. Although he was tired after a long battle, his feet are wounded, clothes are torn, even then there is so much peace and shine on his face. He has a sword in his right hand and ready to pounce on the enemy and to face any danger. The iron ring tied around the turban is a symbol of coming from the battlefield and ready for battle. The jungle scene is at its best, there are different types of trees, plants, cactus plants, etc. A snake is shown with its raised hood as if to provide shade from some of the danger in the forest. Birds, insects are shown busy in their daily activities. An evil-looking big tree is symbolic of the combined forces chasing the Guru. All the sufferings and difficulties can never touch him. Here he rested for a while. Some cactus plants have small beautiful flowers blooming, symbolic of hope. Hope, courage, and willpower to fight any impending danger were the virtues the Guru always infused in the Sikhs.

ਯਾਰੜੇ ਦਾ ਸਾਨੂੰ ਸਥਰ ਚੰਗਾ ਭੱਠ ਖੇੜਿਆਂ ਦਾ ਰਹਿਣਾ।

The Guru in this Shabad yearns for remembrance of WaheGuru despite extreme hardship & tough times rather than living comfortably without WaheGuru's name.

The Artist completed this painting in 1950 and a devotee from Russia purchased it.

ALAMGIR

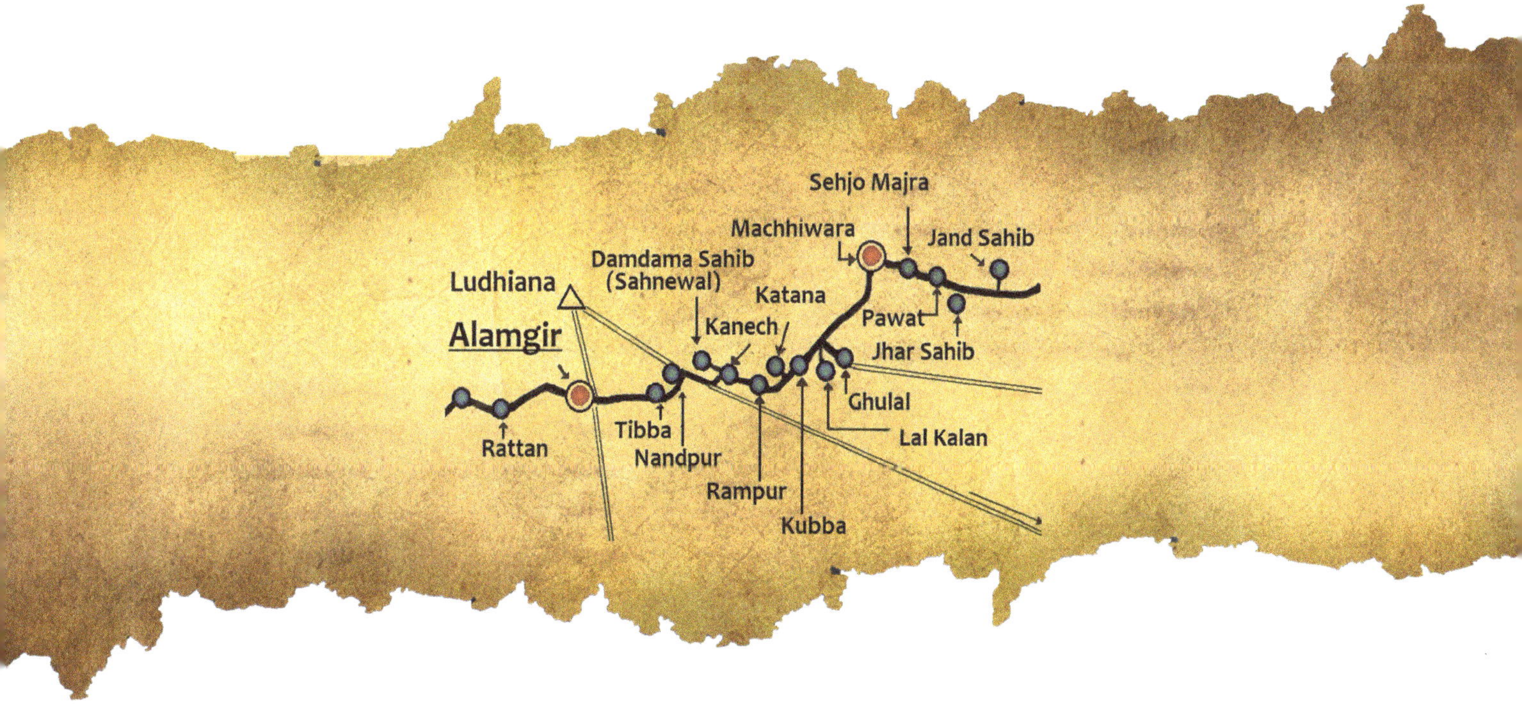

Two Pathan brothers Gani Khan and Nabi Khan, devout followers of Guru Gobind Singh, helped the Guru to move out of Machhiwara as *Pir of Uch*.

When they reached Lal Kalan near Ghulal, again the search party stopped the Guru and his companions. They were asked to partake food. The *Pir* excused himself, saying that he was on fast. His companions ate the food after offering the food to holy Kirpan. For further identification, Qazi Pir Mohammad was called upon. He lived nearby in Nurpur. He had earlier taught Persian to the Guru at Anandpur Sahib. He came and identified that the person in the Palanquin was *Uch Da Pir*. The search party allowed them to move further.

Crossing Kubba, Katana, Rampur, Kanecha, Nandpur, Tibba, they reached Alamgir. It was here, the Guru discarded the special palanquin and took a horse which was presented to him by Bhai Naudh Singh, a horse trader, and resident of Alamgir. The place where Gani Khan and Nabi Khan bid farewell to the Guru exists the Gurdwara *Manji Sahib* in the village Alamgir in Ludhiana District. The Guru blessed them as his own Farzands and gave *Hukamnama* (an autographed letter addressed to all the Sikhs). Gani Khan and Nabi Khan were permitted to go back to their house. The Guru also gave a pair of gold bracelets to the brave Pathans. It is still preserved with their descendants. A photocopy of *Hukamnama* is preserved at Gurdwara Sahib Sri Gani Khan and Nabi Khan at Machhiwara.

On reaching there, the Guru asked the Sikhs to bring water but the villagers complained that water in the well was contaminated. The Guru shot an arrow into the ground where a spring of drinking water sprang up. At this place, Gurdwara *Tir Sahib* has been built.

The Artist completed this painting in 1952

Guru Gobind Singh as '*Uch Da Pir*'

ਉਚੱ ਦਾ ਪੀਰ

In the painting, the Artist has shown Guru's sitting style as that of a great Muslim saint with hair covered with blue cloth but complete alertness on the face. The Guru is shown sitting on a *Manji* lifted on shoulders the way a great Muslim saint is taken with great respect from one place to another. They dressed the Guru in a blue robe as worn by Muslim Fakirs. Gani Khan, Nabi Khan, Bhai Man Singh, Bhai Daya Singh, and Bhai Dharm Singh accompanied the Guru. Whoever questioned them on the way was told that they were carrying '*Uch Da Pir*' (a high Muslim Saint) a *Pir* from a place *Uch*, near Multan. Guru's Persian tutor Qazi Pir Mohammad was called at the check post. He identified the Guru as *Uch Da Pir* and later accompanied them. This way they took the Guru to a safe place. In the background, scenery is of the local area of that place.

Guru Gobind Singh as *'Uch Da Pir'*
ਉਚੱ ਦਾ ਪੀਰ

ਜਬ ਆਵ ਕੀ ਅਉਧ ਨਿਦਾਨ ਬਨੈ ਅਤਿ ਹੀ ਰਨ ਮੇ ਤਬ ਜੂਝ ਮਰੋਂ।।

The Guru says that when his mortal life comes to an end, he would like to die fighting courageously for noble cause.

VILLAGE MOHI

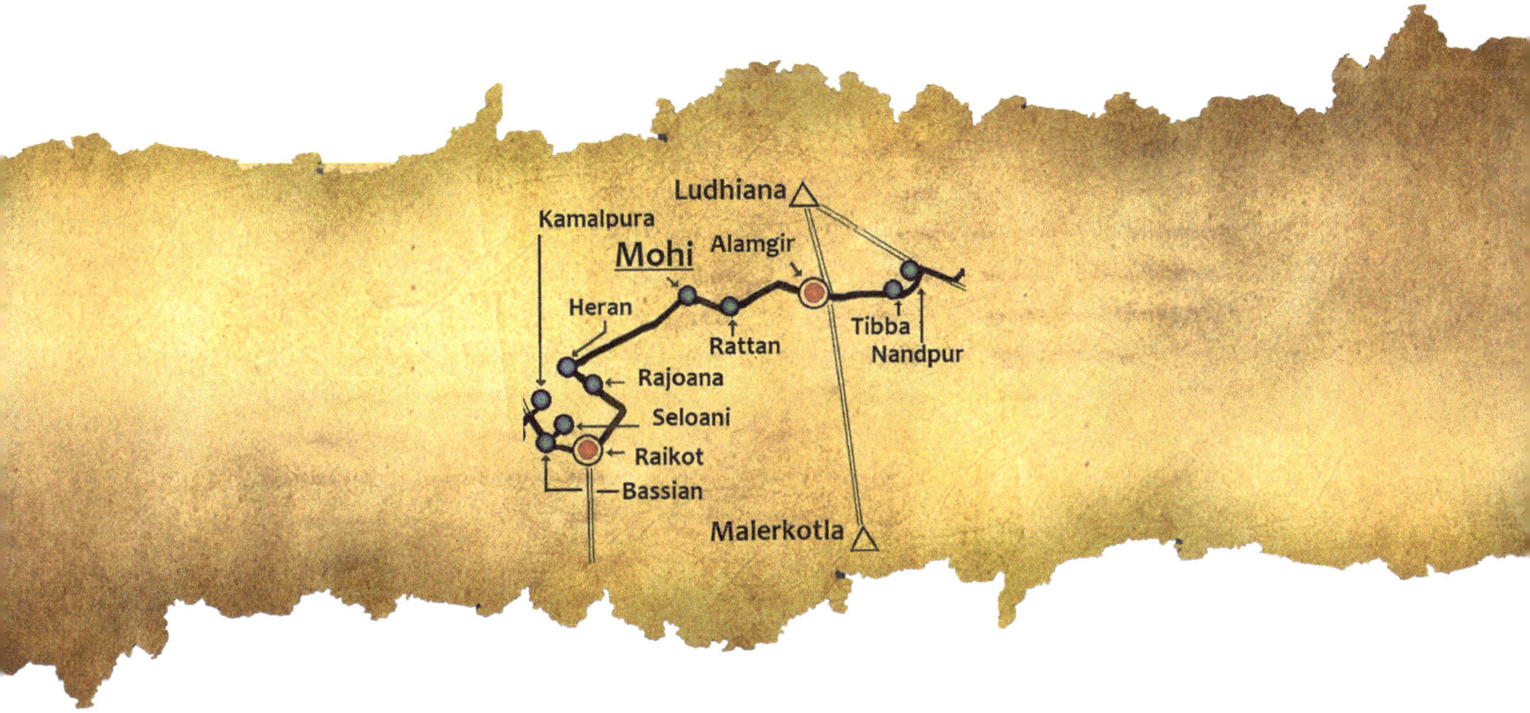

Guru Gobind Singh took the horse presented by his Sikh devotee of Alamgir and moved ahead.

The Guru and Sikhs reached village Mohi and stayed for a night. The Guru came to a blacksmith's workshop and asked him to cut down a tight ring from his finger. The Guru was quite pleased with the job done by the blacksmith. Happily, the Guru asked him if he wanted some favour in return. The blacksmith, Bhai Jawala Singh said that he was afraid that his sons might not have children as nobody is ready to give his daughter in marriage. Guru blessed him that his sons will be married twice. The Guru blessed him with the ring, and the same is still with his descendants.

After getting the ring cut from the blacksmith of Village Mohi, the Guru moved ahead.

Guru Gobind Singh is getting his tight ring cut from blacksmith's workshop.

Guru Gobind Singh, fully armoured, is shown sitting on a small cot in a traditional blacksmith's workshop. His sitting posture has been shown of a brave soldier in active position (Veer Asana). He has his bow in one hand. Blacksmith is cutting the ring keeping it on the anvil with a hammer and a chisel. In the traditional shop, a charcoal furnace has been shown in operation with one person on bellow to pump air in the furnace. In the furnace, iron is heated-up and is used to make various equipment. A variety of tools like anvil, hammer, chisel and other agriculture appliances are scattered as shown in the painting. The mud houses, doors, a three-legged stool and village life are shown. Guru Gobind Singh's horse is also shown in the picture.

Guru was quite pleased with the job done by the blacksmith. The Artist visited village Mohi and met the descendants of the blacksmith before making this painting ready. Village Mohi has also been depicted in the painting. It can be seen from the blacksmith's workshop. Villagers are shown busy in their daily chores.

RAIKOT

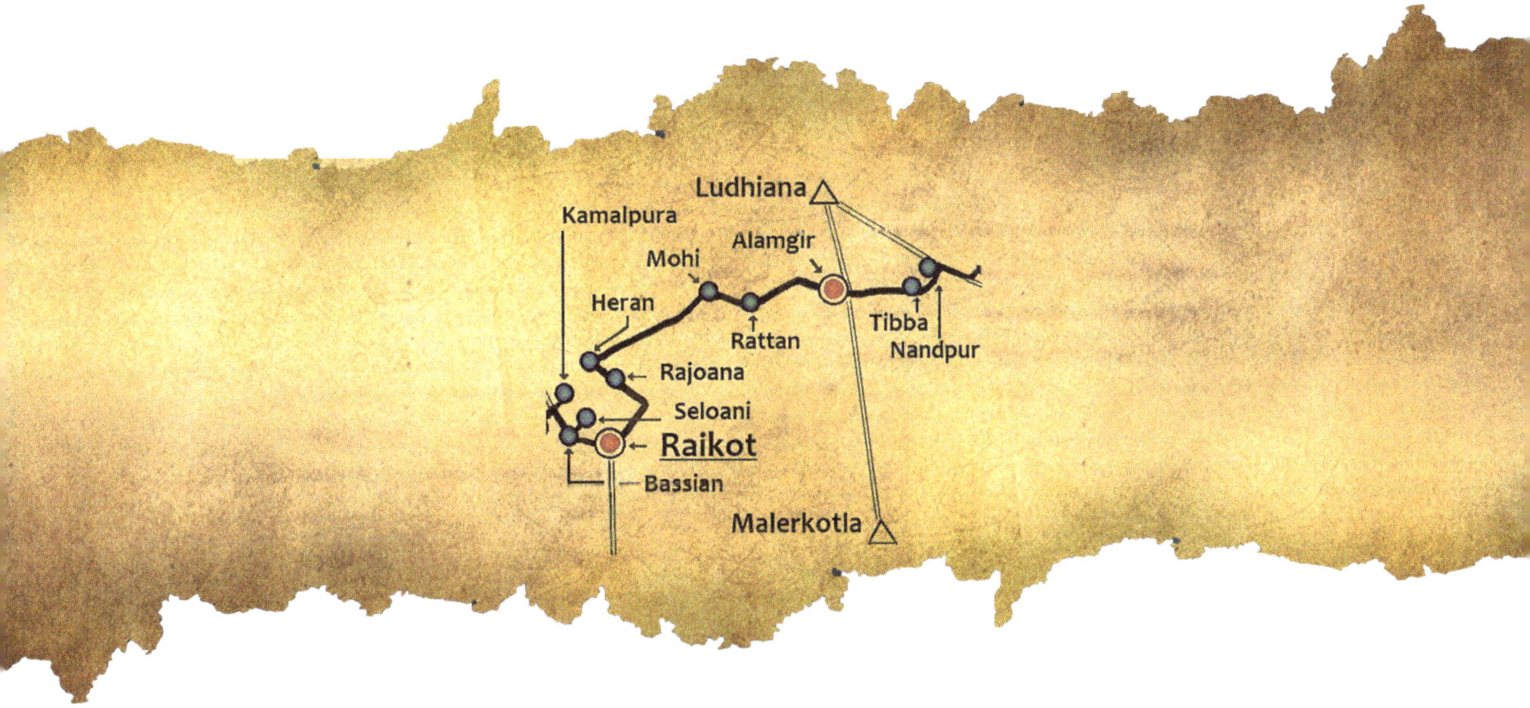

Guru Gobind Singh uprooting Kahi (Shrub) at Raikot symbolising the fall of Mughal Empire

Guru Gobind Singh had his tight finger ring cut in village Mohi and proceeded further. He reached village Hehar and met Kirpal, a successor of Udassi Mahant, who had fought valiantly in the battle of Bhangani at Paonta Sahib and crushed the head of a deserted Pathan Hayat Khan. The mahant welcomed the Guru and the Sikhs.

From Hehar, the Guru proceeded towards Raikot. Rai Kalha was the local ruler of the village Raikot. He was a Muslim born but was a great devotee of the Guru. He came and took the Guru to his house with respect and love.

Rai Kalha offered his services to the Guru. The Guru asked him to send someone to enquire from Sarhind about his two sons Zorawar Singh and Fateh Singh and his mother, Mata Gujri, who had been separated from him at Privar Vichora. Rai Kalha sent a messenger named Noora Mahi to Sarhind to find out what had happened to Mata Gujri and the younger sons.

When Mahi came back and narrated the painful happenings of Sarhind, Rai Kalha and the rest of people were moved to tears. The Guru thanked the Almighty God. The Guru was sitting and with the tip of his arrow, he was digging the root of a shrub (*Kahi*). Then, the Guru said that soon the Mughal rulers, like the shrub, would be uprooted and the town of Sarhind has invited its own doom. The martyred Sahibzadas have infused new life into the dead bones of the people.

Then Rai Kalha pleaded that he being a Muslim, should be saved from the ire of the Lord. The Guru blessed him and told him that he has saved himself as he truly loved humanity. The Guru gave him his *Ganga Sagar (*a copper urn having symmetrical holes around the circumference), sword, and *Rehal* (wooden holy book stand) as a token of Guru's love for him.

Rai Kalha's descendants left for Pakistan in 1947.

ਕੋਊ ਭਇਓ ਮੁੰਡੀਆ ਸੰਨਿਆਸੀ ਕੋਊ ਜੋਗੀ ਭਇਓ ਕੋਊ ਬ੍ਰਹਮਚਾਰੀ ਕੋਊ ਜਤੀ ਅਨੁਮਾਨਬੋ।
ਹਿੰਦੂ ਤੁਰਕ ਕੋਊ ਰਾਫਜੀ ਇਮਾਮ ਸਾਫੀ ਮਾਨਸ ਕੀ ਜਾਤਿ ਸਬੈ ਏਕੈ ਪਹਿਚਾਨਬੋ।
ਕਰਤਾ ਕਰੀਮ ਸੋਈ ਰਾਜਕ ਰਹੀਮ ਓਈ ਦੂਸਰੋ ਨ ਭੇਦ ਕੋਈ ਭੂਲਿ ਭ੍ਰਮ ਮਾਨਬੋ।
ਏਕ ਹੀ ਕੀ ਸੇਵ ਸਭ ਹੀ ਕੋ ਗੁਰਦੇਵ ਏਕ ਏਕ ਹੀ ਸਰੂਪ ਸਬੈ ਏਕੈ ਜੋਤ ਜਾਨਬੋ।।

Some are Hindus (Yogis, Brahamchari, Jati, Sanyasi) and some are
Muslims (Shia, Sunni) but still they belong to one race i.e. Human beings.
The Almighty God is the Creator, Sustainer, Merciful,
Compassionate, there is none else. The Almighty God is
the only reality. All human beings are His children.

DINA-KANGAR

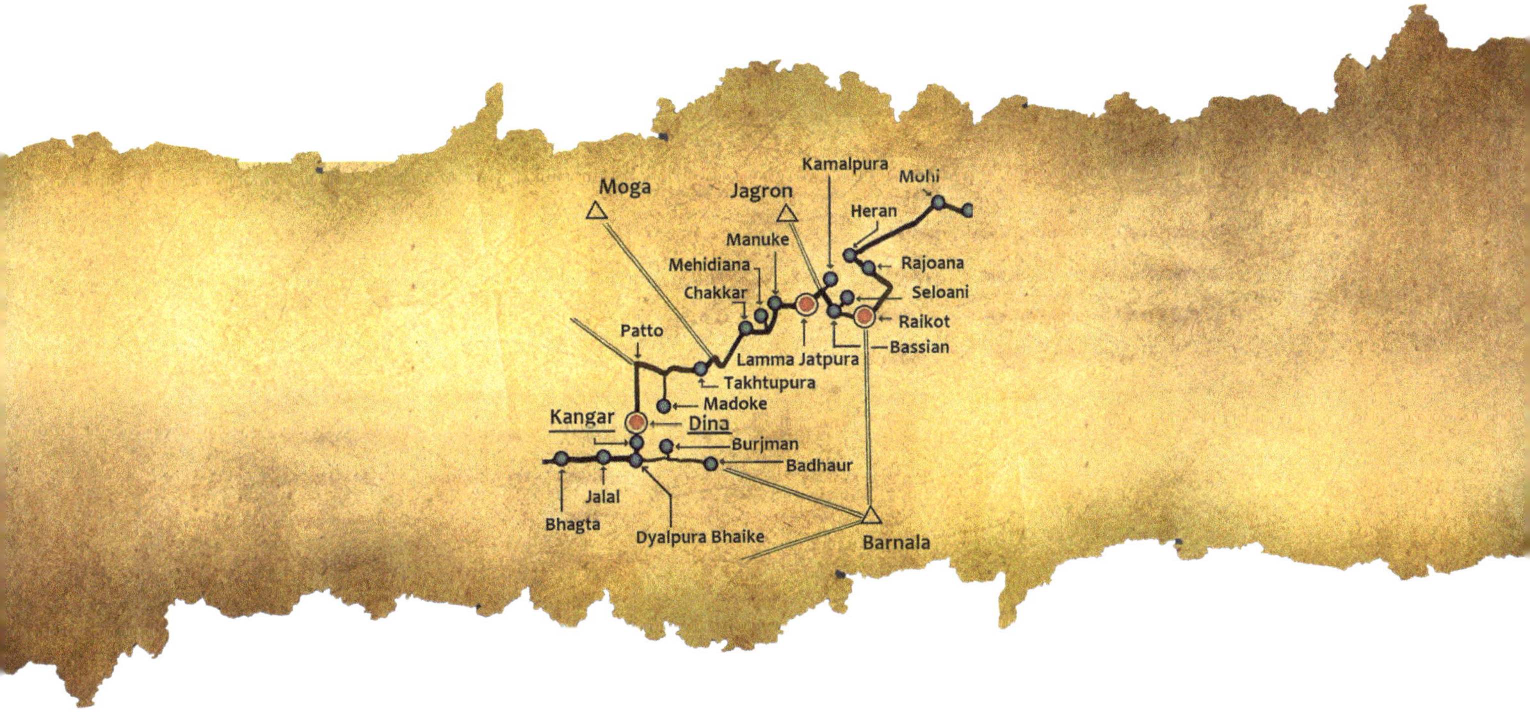

Wrote Zafarnama at Dina

From Raikot, Guru Gobind Singh moved forward and reached Dina-Kangar. He was welcomed there by three brothers Shamira, Lakhmira, and Takhat Mal. Knowing the risk of looking after him, the three brothers told the Guru that they were ready to sacrifice everything for the Guru. The Guru stayed at this place for quite some time. People started coming to this place to have his blessings.

Here, Guru Gobind Singh wrote his famous victory letter in Persian to Aurangzeb. He called it 'Zafarnama' means ' The Epistle of Victory'.

In Zafarnama, the Guru confirmed his confidence and unflinching faith in the Almighty God even after suffering extreme personal loss. Guru put himself as a firm believer in Almighty God, a tough fighter for righteousness and Aurangzeb as cruel, treacherous, inhuman, and cunning like a fox. The Guru wrote that he has no trust in Aurangzeb's solemn oaths taken on Quran anymore, and that his generals are all liars.

The Guru also gave an account of the battle of Chamkaur Sahib that ten lakh combined Hill-Rajas and Mughal forces pounced a surprise attack on forty hungry men with swords, arrows and guns after breaking oath on Quran. The Guru was left with no choice and was forced to pick up the sword to fight. The Guru wrote that God Almighty Himself had brought him out from Chamkaur Sahib without a scratch on his body or twist of his hair.

In the letter of victory to Aurangzeb, the Guru happily justified the battle and wrote that when all the means for justice have failed and no hope is in sight, it is then rightful to take up sword (ਚੂੰ ਕਾਰ ਅਜ਼ ਹਮਾਂ ਹੀਲਤੇ ਦਰ ਗੁਜ਼ੱਸ਼ਤ। ਹਲਾਲ ਅਸਤ ਬੁਰਦਨ ਬ ਸ਼ਮਸ਼ੀਰ ਦਸਤ।). The 'sword' symbolising *Shakti* was not to be used as a butcher's knife but as a surgeon's instrument to root out the tyrannies.

The Guru wrote that there was no difference on account that his four sons have been killed, the coiled cobra (Khalsa) still remained behind. He warned Aurangzeb to stop torturing the weak and timid with royal military might. The Guru invited Aurangzeb to Kangar to meet him for redemption.

Bhai Dharam Singh and Bhai Daya Singh, the two surviving beloved ones, were sent to deliver the Zafarnama to Aurangzeb. The Emperor read the letter and felt that the Guru was a highly intelligent, truthful and fearless warrior. Aurangzeb regretted at what he had done in his lifetime and sent a letter to the Guru requesting him to meet him in Ahmadnagar at his earliest convenience.

Aurangzeb admitted in his Will that his inner soul is cursing him, but of no avail. He died and the meeting never took place.

Saviour of Mankind - Guru Gobind Singh - ਦੇਸ਼, ਦੀਨ ਦੇ ਵਾਲੀ ਸ੍ਰੀ ਦਸ਼ਮੇਸ਼ ਜੀ

This historic painting by S. Trilok Singh Artist is based upon poet Mansa Singh Dukhi's poem. This poem is also in Mahan kosh of Bhai Kahan Singh Nabha. The word *Bar* 'ਬਾਰ' has been used in eighteen different ways. Guru Gobind Singh's whole life has been described in the short poem.

ਬਾਰ ਤਨ ਮਨ ਧਨ ਗੋਬਿੰਦ ਮ੍ਰਿਗਿੰਦ ਪਾਂਹਿ, ਬੈਰਿਨ ਕੋ ਬਾਰ ਬਾਰਿ ਹਿੰਦਨ ਕੀ ਬਾਰ ਕੀ,
ਬਾਰ ਥੀ ਉਮਰ ਬਾਰ ਬੈਰਿਨ ਕੇ ਪਠਿਯੋ ਬਾਪ, ਬਾਰ ਦੀਨੋ ਸੀਸ ਹਿਤ ਦੇਸ਼ ਸਮ ਬਾਰ ਕੀ,
ਬਾਰ ਬਾਰ ਚਾਰ ਨਾਉ ਕੌਮ ਕੀ ਉਬਾਰ ਲੀਨੀ, ਬੂਡਤੀ ਥੀ ਬਾਰ ਨਾ ਲਗਾਈ ਬਾਰ ਬਾਰ ਕੀ,
ਬਾਰ ਤੇ ਅਨੇਕ ਬਾਰ ਚੂਕਤ ਅਚੂਕ ਪਿਤਾ, ਹੁਜੀਓ ਕ੍ਰਿਪਾਲ ਮੇਰੀ ਬਾਰ ਕੇਹੀ ਬਾਰ ਕੀ।

Verse / Meaning	No.	Punjabi	English
ਬਾਰ[1] ਤਨ ਮਨ ਧਨ ਗੋਬਿੰਦ ਮ੍ਰਿਗਿੰਦ ਪਾਂਹਿ ਬੈਰਿਨ ਕੋ **ਬਾਰ**[2] **ਬਾਰਿ**[3] ਹਿੰਦਨ ਕੀ **ਬਾਰ**[4] ਕੀ।।	1. **ਬਾਰ**[1]	**ਕੁਰਬਾਨ**	Sacrifice
Guru Gobind Singh sacrificed everything for the sake of mankind and motherland. He stood fearlessly to protect the motherland against tyrants.	2. **ਬਾਰ**[2] 3. **ਬਾਰਿ**[3] 4. **ਬਾਰ**[4]	ਜਾਲ (ਜਲਨਾ) ਫੁਲਵਾੜੀ ਵਾੜ	burn Garden Fence
ਬਾਰ[5] ਥੀ ਉਮਰ **ਬਾਰ**[6] ਬੈਰਿਨ ਕੇ ਪਠਿਯੋ ਬਾਪ, **ਬਾਰ**[7] ਦੀਨੋ ਸੀਸ ਹਿਤ ਦੇਸ਼ ਸਮ **ਬਾਰ**[8] ਕੀ।।	5. **ਬਾਰ**[5] 6. **ਬਾਰ**[6]	ਬਚਪਨ ਦਰਵਾਜਾ	Childhood Door
In childhood, he sent his father, Guru Teg Bahadur, being a true holy person, to the Mughal Emperor to stop forcible conversion of Hindus to Islam. His father made the supreme sacrifice of his head for the sake of motherland accepting death and maintained honour.	7. **ਬਾਰ**[7] 8. **ਬਾਰ**[8] 9. **ਬਾਰ**[9]	ਵਾਰਨਾ, ਕੁਰਬਨ ਵਾਲ (ਕੇਸ) ਵਾਰਕੇ	Sacrifice Hair Sacrificed
ਬਾਰ[9] **ਬਾਰ**[10] ਚਾਰ ਨਾਉ ਕੌਮ ਕੀ **ਉਬਾਰ**[11] ਲੀਨੀ ਬੂਡਤੀ ਥੀ **ਬਾਰ**[12] ਨਾ ਲਗਾਈ **ਬਾਰ**[13] **ਬਾਰ**[14] ਕੀ।।	10. **ਬਾਰ**[10] 11. **ਬਾਰ**[11]	ਲਾਲ (ਬੱਚੇ) ਕੱਢਣੀ	Children, Sons to take out
Time and again, he fought fearlessly with tyrants and evil-minded rulers. He sacrificed his four sons to save the sinking ship of the nation. He didn't waste any time. By sacrificing everything he had, he took the ship to its destination safely.	12. **ਬਾਰ**[12] 13. **ਬਾਰ**[13] 14. **ਬਾਰ**[14]	ਸਮੁੰਦਰ ਦੇਰੀ ਬਾਹਰ ਕੀਤਾ	Sea Delay Take to shore
ਬਾਰ[15] ਤੋ ਅਨੇਕ **ਬਾਰ**[16] ਚੂਕਤ ਅਚੂਕ ਪਿਤਾ ਹੁਜੀਓ ਕਿਰਪਾਲ ਮੇਰੀ **ਬਾਰ**[17] ਕੇਹੀ **ਬਾਰ**[18] ਕੀ।।	15. **ਬਾਰ**[15] 16. **ਬਾਰ**[16]	ਬਚੇ ਵਾਰੀ	Saved Again
A child makes mistakes but his father shows him the correct path. The Poet says that dear kind Guru, the saviour of mankind, why he is taking too much time, on his turn.	17. **ਬਾਰ**[17] 18. **ਬਾਰ**[18]	ਵਾਰੀ ਦੇਰੀ	Turn Delay

At a very young age, Gobind Rai sacrificed his father for the cause of Dharma. Aurangzeb had ordered that all Hindus should be converted to Islam. Kashmiri Pandits, being learned and most respected, became his target. A group of Pandits came to Guru Teg Bahadur to seek help in their hour of need. The Guru explained that sacrifice of a truly holy man could save them. Gobind Rai suggested that who else can be holier than Guru Teg Bahadur for this noble cause. At such an early age, Guru Gobind Singh sacrificed his father for the freedom of faith.

Guru Teg Bahadur readied himself for the journey to Delhi along with Bhai Mati Das, Bhai Sati Das, Bhai Dayal Das. He was asked to perform miracle or accept Islam, but the Guru refused. Then he was asked to choose between Islam and death. Guru Teg Bahadur accepted death. He believed in the freedom of faith so he attained martyrdom. Guru Teg Bahadur made the supreme sacrifice for the sake of protecting the Hindu religion.

The Artist has drawn a map of India with Guru Teg Bhadur's head lying on it. The Guru sacrificed himself for the nation. He stood for freedom of faith for all human beings. He has truly been called *'Srishti Di Chadar'*, protector of the people. He gave up his life to protect and defend the individual rights to follow the religion of one's choice.

Guru's four sons attained martyrdom in December 1704, two younger ones at Sarhind, and two elder ones at Chamkaur Sahib.

At Privar Vichora, while crossing river Sirsa, Mata Gujri, with two younger grandsons, got separated from the Guru and the Sikhs. Then they met Gangu Brahmin, who had been a cook in their house. He took them to his house and later, handed them over to the Subedar of Sarhind. Wazir Khan asked the young ones to accept Islam or death. But they bravely and fearlessly refused to accept Islam. Then he ordered to brick them alive. They attained martyrdom at the tender age.

The battle of Chamkaur Sahib is very unique in the history of mankind. On the one hand, there were forty Sikhs and Guru Gobind Singh, along with his two elder sons. On the other hand, there were 10 lakh soldiers of Hill-Rajas and Mughals. In the battle, Guru's two sons Ajit Singh and Jujhar Singh attained martyrdom while fighting bravely. Nowhere in history, a father has himself sent his sons to the battlefield – unto a sure death. He saw them fighting fiercely and meeting death. Then the Guru thanked the Almighty.

In the painting, the Artist has shown Guru Gobind Singh taking the ship of mankind towards the destination against all odds. People belonging to different castes, creeds, high or low are in the ship symbolizing Guru's love for all. All were equal in his eyes. He prayed to God to die fighting for a good cause.

The atrocities of the Emperor and Rajas were at its peak, and the conversion campaign was also in full swing. The ship of religion, as shown in the painting, was facing difficulties. It was in turbulent waters. It may or may not reach the shore. The Guru came as the saviour of mankind. He sacrificed all his sons at the tender age. He helped the ship of religion to reach the shore safely.

The Guru created a fence around the country. He created Khalsa Panth. He raised an army of brave soldiers who were ready to face the challenges thrown by the Mughals by sacrificing his father at a very young age. He showed that he was not afraid of the mighty Emperor. He was fearless and brave as a lion. A lion has been shown in the painting as a symbol of bravery. No odds or difficulties could dampen his spirits. He was always in high spirits to encourage and infuse confidence in his devotees, even in the battlefield. He created a fence around the country. 'Hindan ki var' as shown by the Artist.

Guru Gobind Singh wrote Zafarnama, 'The Epistle of Victory' to Aurangzeb. In the letter, he has written about all the atrocities unleashed by the Mughal Emperor on the innocent, weak, and the downtrodden masses. He was not afraid of the Emperor. He told the Emperor in straight words that he was not true to his words. The Guru had firm faith in Almighty God. He always prayed to God to give him strength and courage to help fellow human beings. He also prayed to God to die in the battlefield fighting for noble and good deeds. He is the true saviour of mankind. He sacrificed everything he had for the benefit of mankind.

The Guru wrote in Zafarnama, "What if you have killed my four sons, the cobra is still alive." The Artist has shown a hawk killing a small snake. Here, the hawk is symbolic of the mighty Mughal Emperor and the small snake symbolic of the weaker section of society. The Artist has shown a coiled snake hunting the hawk. The coiled snake is symbolic of Khalsa Panth created by the Tenth Guru. The Khalsa has courage, determination and strong willpower to strike at the very root of the Mughal Empire. Later, the Mughal Empire was uprooted by Khalsa.

At the bottom left side, the Artist has shown Bharat Mata offering thanks to the Guru for saving her honour and helping humanity in the hour of need.

On the right side, the Artist has shown himself as an ignorant child seeking the Guru's blessing to enlighten his mind.

MUKATSAR

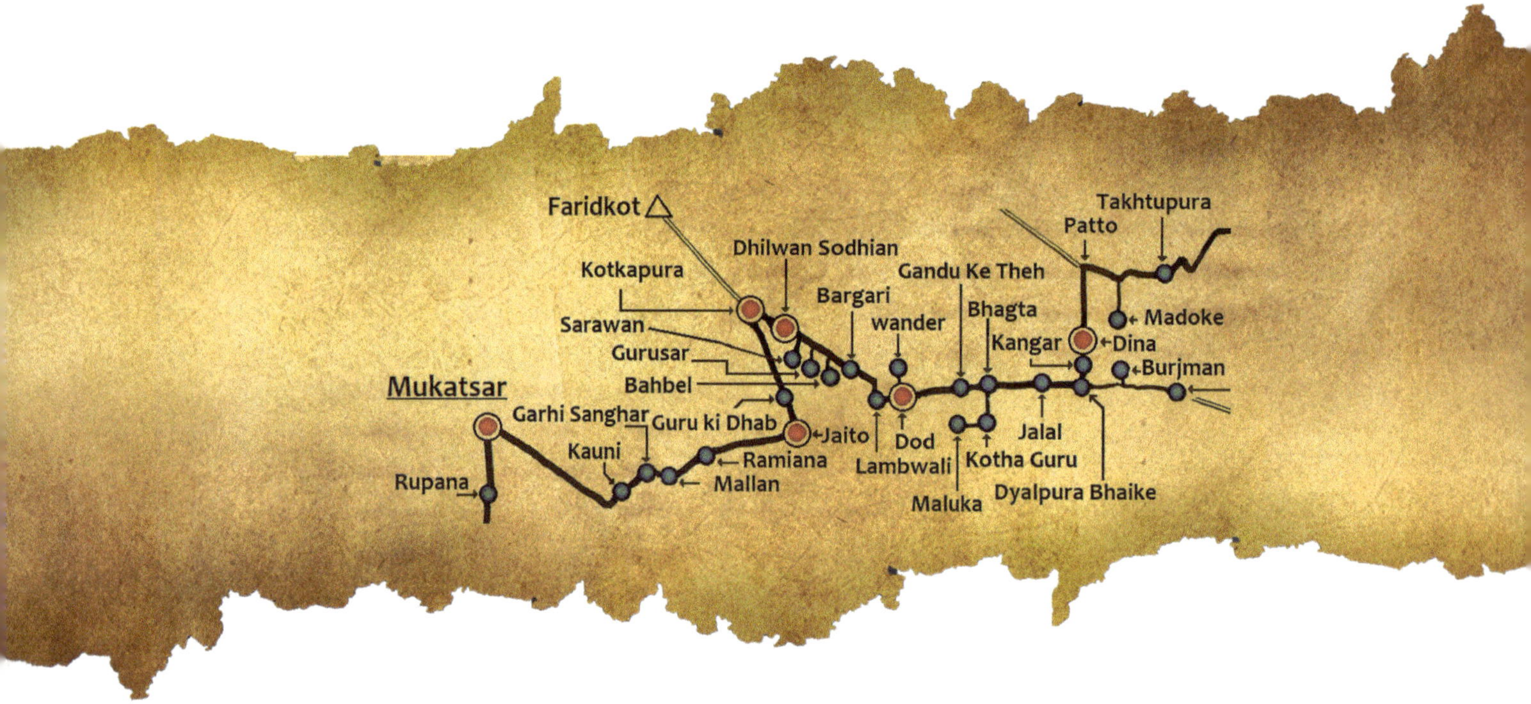

Tearing off the *bedaba* of the forty and made them *Muktas* - the saved ones.

Guru Gobind Singh stayed at Dina-Kangar for some time. Many volunteers and paid Sikhs assembled around the the Guru. Then travelling through Jalal, Bhagata, and several other villages, the Guru and the Sikhs arrived near Kot Kapura forest. A Sikh brought the news that Wazir Khan is coming with over 5000 soldiers. Kapura of Kot Kapura refused to let the Guru use his fortress for the fight with enemy.

Guru moved further and reached Khidrana *Dhab (a lake)* as the place of battle. Many devoted Sikhs were prepared to face the enemy.

The Sikhs who had deserted the Guru at Anandpur Sahib at a crucial time, had been ashamed by their families. So these Sikhs decided to fight for the Guru. They met the Guru near Khidrana. Many other devotees also joined them on the way with weapons. Bhai Mahan Singh proposed to engage the army there and thus allow the Guru to reach a place of safety. They placed big white sheets (*Chadar*) on the shrubs so that the enemy might think that Sikhs were camping there in great numbers.

Soon the Mughal armies reached there, a fierce battle was fought between the Sikhs and the Mughals. The Guru meanwhile camped at a nearby mound. He directed a rain of arrows killing a large number of enemy soldiers. About 3000 soldiers were killed, the Mughals took over the possession of the lake of Khidrana and found it dry. Frustrated at losing so many men, Wazir Khan retreated.

The Guru visited the place of the battle and with fatherly affection, was lifting the heads of martyrs. Then he saw that Bhai Mahan Singh was still alive. He lifted his head and placed the head in his lap. The Guru asked him if he had any wish. Mahan Singh was filled with Supreme love. He asked that the Guru should bless all the forty deserters by tearing off the *Bedaba* (a disclaimer letter) written by them. The Guru was highly pleased. He blessed all, took the letter of disclaimer from under his belt and tore it off. He told Mahan Singh that all the forty are *Muktas* - the saved ones. They are saved from the cycle of birth and death. Mai Bhago had also fought bravely. Later on, she was baptised as Mai Bhag Kaur and served the Guru till the end.

The tank of Khidrana was named as Mukatsar i.e. tank of salvation. Every year on the first of the month of Magh, Sikhs gather there to remember the brave martyrs of Mukatsar.

This painting is based on the Gurbani lines taken from Dasam Granth by the Tenth Guru.

The Artist has beautifully illustrated the ideals and beliefs of the Tenth Guru.

Guru Gobind Singh completed the work started by the first Guru - Guru Nanak Dev. The social conditions at the time of the birth of the first Guru were at its lowest ebb. Guru Nanak laid the foundation of a new religion which would enable the people to stand erect against the oppressors. They would lead householder's lives and still remain detached from worldly attractions as the lotus grows in muddy water and remains unaffected by the dirt around it. The Tenth Guru completed the work of raising a new kind of people free from the curse of the caste system. He infused courage and confidence in the people to stand up against tyrannies of Mughal Empire.

Vanquisher of the Enemy - (ਗ਼ਨੀਮੁਲ ਸ਼ਿਕਸਤੈ ॥) The Guru created the Khalsa – an army of saint-soldiers. By drinking the nectar, the weak ones became brave and courageous. The lowly became at par with the upper caste. The persons, who had never touched a sword or any other weapon, showed marvellous courage and bravery in the battlefield that stunned the Mughal forces.

Protector of the weaker section - (ਗ਼ਰੀਬੁਲ ਪਰਸਤੈ ॥) The Guru protected the weaker section of the society and acted as their shield.

Most importantly, he wanted to kill the negative qualities of a person 'Fear not, Frighten not' was always his motto for the Sikhs. He wanted the Sikhs to be truthful, brave and courageous so that they could lead the life of dignity. He wanted to save the poor people from the clutches of atrocities unleashed by the rulers. He had immense love for human beings as they are the children of the same Supreme God. (ਏਕ ਪਿਤਾ ਏਕਸ ਕੇ ਹਮ ਬਾਰਿਕ। ।)

At the bottom of the painting, the Artist has written ਵਿਦਿਆ, ਵਿਜੈ, ਵਿਨੈ, ਵੀਰਤਾ। ਵਾਹੁ ਵਾਹੁ ਗੋਬਿੰਦ ਸਿੰਘ ॥ ... The Guru always laid stress on these qualities.

Education - (ਵਿਦਿਆ) The Guru himself was Arabic, Persian, Sanskrit, Brij Bhasha and Gurumukhi scholar. His poetry in these languages is par excellence. Poets, scholars and musicians were always held in high esteem by the Guru.

Victory - (ਵਿਜੈ) The Hill-Rajas and the Mughals thrust so many battles on the Guru. He was always victorious in them but he always thanked the Almighty God for his victories and praised the Khalsa for fighting bravely in battles.

Humility - (ਵਿਨੈ) The Guru was humility personified. He always called himself the mere servant of the Supreme God who has just come to see the drama of life. (ਮੈ ਹੋ ਪਰਮ ਪੁਰਖ ਕੋ ਦਾਸਾ। ਦੇਖਨਿ ਆਯੋ ਜਗਤ ਤਮਾਸਾ ॥)

Bravery - (ਵੀਰਤਾ) The Guru was brave and fearless like a lion. He had vowed to make the sparrows hunt the falcon, to make one fight lakhs. He succeeded in this impossible task. (ਨਿਸਚੈ ਕਰ ਅਪਨੀ ਜੀਤ ਕਰੋਂ ॥)

MUKATSAR

Baba Banda Singh Bahadar, a mere yogi, drank the nectar (ਪੀਓ ਪਾਹੁਲ ਖੰਡੇ ਧਾਰ। ।) and came like a whirlwind to uproot the Mughal Empire.

The Guru created an army of brave men who were ready to die for noble and righteous deeds. They always prayed to die in the battlefield fighting for a noble cause.

Guru Gobind Singh created Khalsa. He prepared Amrit and baptised the five who became the beloved five. Then he asked the five to baptise him. Thus, he became the Guru as well as the Disciple. (ਵਾਹੁ ਵਾਹੁ ਗੋਬਿੰਦ ਸਿੰਘ ਆਪੇ ਗੁਰ ਚੇਲਾ॥)

At Nanded, he named Guru Granth Sahib as the Guru.

Artist Trilok Singh explaining Giani Zail Singh, Chief Minister, Punjab, the life of Guru Gobind Singh depicted in ninteen stars in the painting at his residence 'Chitralok' Patiala – 1973.

CHHATIANA
(GUPTSAR - A HIDDEN TREASURE)

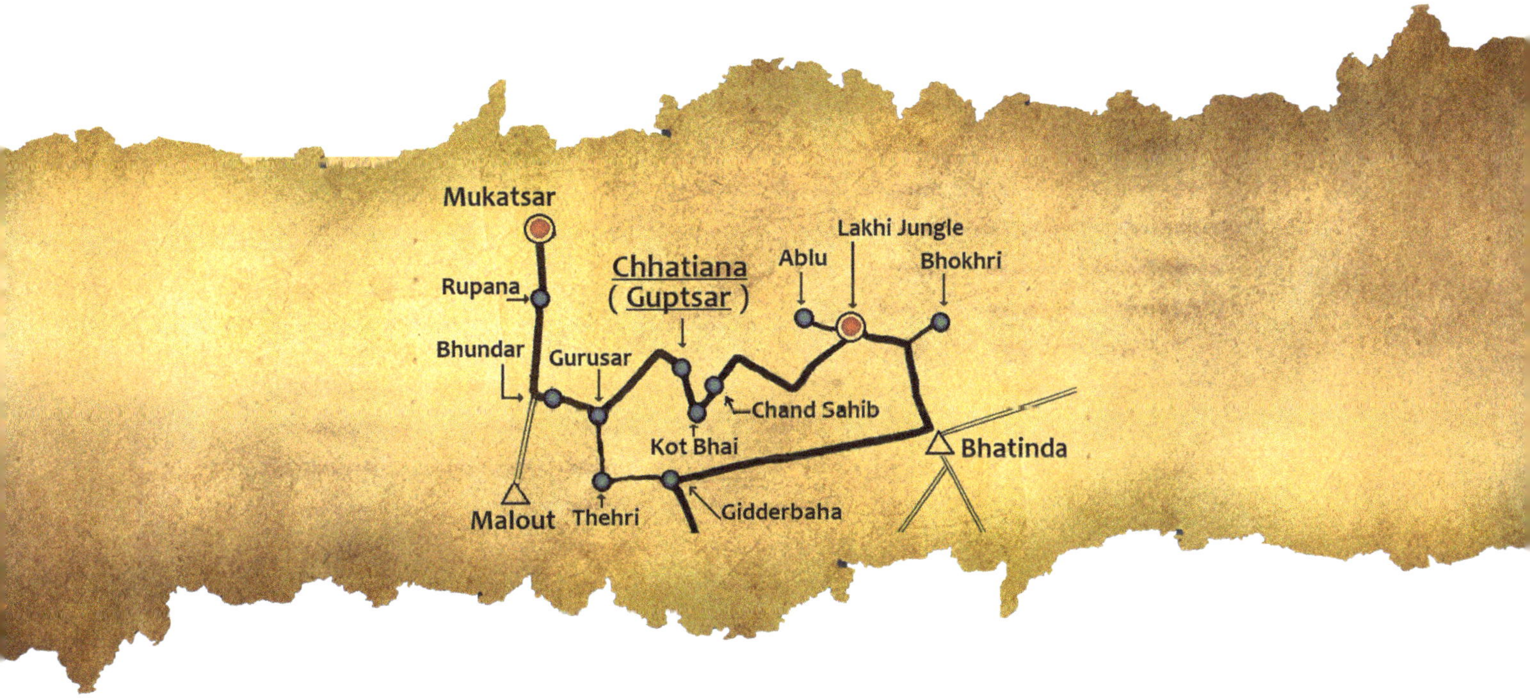

Guptsar

After the battle of Mukatsar, Guru Gobind Singh continued his journey through Rupana, Bhundar, and Gurusar and reached Chhatiana. More and more people kept on following the Guru, getting his blessings.

In addition to Guru's voluntary saint-soldiers, the Guru had engaged a large number of Sikhs from the Malwa area, mostly Brars, as his paid soldiers. They could not be paid regularly. After some time, they started complaining. They asked the Guru to clear their accounts.

At Chhatiana, they became impatient and asked the Guru to give them their wages, there and then. They refused to allow the Guru to move further till the wages were paid. The Guru told them to wait for some more time as he had no money at that time. The Guru told them to have faith in God and wait for some more time. But they refused to listen to the Guru. Just then, a Sikh arrived with large sacks of gold and silver coins and placed them at the Guru's feet.

The Guru told the Brar soldiers to come one by one and take their wages. Most of the Brar soldiers went away after taking their salaries. After seeing that Guru has lots of money, they came back and asked for double payment. They were paid double. But their leader, Dana refused to take money and begged the Guru to let him remain with the Guru forever. Guru blessed him and told him that he had preserved the foundation of faith in the Malwa region. Dana drank the nectar and became Dana Singh, a Khalsa.

The remaining money was buried by the Guru at that place. The Guru then moved on and continued his journey baptising the Sikhs and blessing them. After he had left, Brars tried to dig out the buried treasure. In spite of their long and hard search, they could not find it. Gurdwara called Guptsar, the hidden treasure, exists there.

Swami Keshwa Nand, Member Parliament purchased the painting and displayed it in the museum at Sangaria (Raj)–1954

TALWANDI SABO
(DAM DAMA SAHIB)

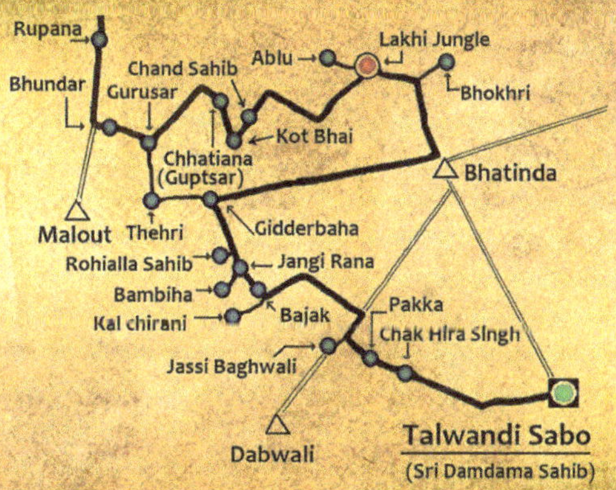

Sri Dam Dama Sahib, Talwandi Sabo, is the fifth Takhat of the Sikhs. After the historic battle of Mukatsar and paying salaries to paid soldiers at Chhatiana, Guru Gobind Singh reached Talwandi Sabo.

Dalla, a disciple of the Guru, was the most prominent resident of Talwandi Sabo. He came with about 400 soldiers to welcome the Guru to his village.

The Guru decided to stop and rest there. The Guru tied his horse with a Kareer tree. A camp was set up there and the place is now called Dam Dama - the breathing or resting place. The news spread around. People started coming to pay respect and get his blessings. The Guru stayed here for about nine months. Soon the place became a center of learning.

The Guru called it the Kashi or Banaras of the Sikhs. Mata Sundri and Mata Sahib Kaur, along with Bhai Mani Singh, came from Delhi and joined the Guru. Mata Sundri enquired about her sons. The Guru replied, “Your four sons have become one with the Supreme Almighty. What if your four sons are killed, millions are still alive.” (ਇਨ ਪੁਤਰਨ ਕੇ ਸੀਸ ਪਰ ਵਾਰ ਦੀਏ ਸੁਤ ਚਾਰ। ਚਾਰ ਮੁਏ ਤੋ ਕਿਆ ਹੁਆ ਜੀਵਤ ਕਈ ਹਜਾਰ।)

The Guru dictated the whole of the Guru Granth Sahib and got it written, the authorised version of Adi Granth, by adding Bani of Guru Teg Bahadur. Bhai Mani Singh wrote it and Baba Deep Singh made four copies of the Holy Granth for the four Takhats.

Gurdwara Damdama Sahib, Likhansar, Manji Sahib are some of the prominent Gurdwaras to commemorate the visit of the Guru to this place. Sacred articles belonging to the Guru, namely sword, mirror, the dress he wore are still preserved there by the descendants of Bhai Dalla.

ਸਾਚੁ ਕਹੋਂ ਸੁਨ ਲੇਹੁ ਸਭੈ ਜਿਨ ਪ੍ਰੇਮ ਕੀਓ ਤਿਨ ਹੀ ਪ੍ਰਭ ਪਾਇਓ।

To tell the truth, listen all – who ever loves Almighty God, achieves the God.

Guru Gobind Singh and Bhai Dalla at Talwandi Sabo

One day a devotee, Bhai Udhey Singh from Lahore brought some new guns and swords for the Guru at Talwandi Sabo. The Guru wanted to test the gun. This is the scene depicted in this painting. The Artist has shown a devotee keeping the gun and sword on the small table. Bhai Dalla had always boasted that his soldiers are ready to lay down their lives for the Guru. The Guru wanted to test the weapon. The Guru asked Dalla to make any soldier as target. When Dalla asked his soldiers to come and be the target, everybody refused. Then the Guru asked his Sikhs to come for the test. The word spread around. Many people started running towards the Guru. Everybody wanted to come first and be the target. Baba Bir Singh and Baba Dhir Singh, father and son, who were tying their turbans, also heard about it and started running. Both of them wanted to be the first person on whom the Guru should take the aim and test the gun. Bhai Dalla is looking astonished to see such devotion. Then the Guru explained that Dalla's soldiers are his paid servants. But Guru's devotees are his beloved Sikhs. They are ever ready to lay down their lives for their Guru. This shows the true love and devotion of his Sikhs.

The Guru's chair, his famous *Baaz* are also shown in the picture. A *Nagara* (a type of a big drum) is also kept on a small table. On one side, people with musical instruments, tabla, rabab are shown performing Gurbani recitation.

Gurdwara DamDama Sahib. After the battle of Mukatsar, Guru Gobind Singh reached Talwandi Sabo. He tied his horse with the Kareer tree (shown in the pic). This tree is preserved in Gurdwara Damdama Sahib. Jotinder Singh Engr-in-chief/ Retd is in the pic.

ਅਨੰਦਪੁਰ ਦੇ ਫੁਰਨੇ
Musings of Anandpur Sahib

After the battle of Mukatsar, Guru Gobind Singh continued his journey in the Malwa area. Passing through many villages, blessing the people on the way, the Guru reached Talwandi Sabo. Dalla, a disciple of the Guru, was the most prominent of the residents. He went to meet the Guru and welcomed him to Talwandi Sabo. Guru Gobind Singh tied his horse to a Kareer tree and asked his Sikhs to put up a tent there so that he could have some rest. Guru Teg Bahadur had also visited this place. The place came to be known as DamDama Sahib meaning the breathing or resting place.

The people in and around Talwandi Sabo used to grow Bajra, Moth and the commonly growing trees were that of Kareer. The area was almost a desert. Dalla used to accompany the Guru where ever he went. The Guru used to say that time would come, the area will have abundance of water to grow crops and other varieties of plants and trees. Dalla never believed all this. He used to tell the Guru that these are all musings of the days he had spent in Anandpur Sahib. No one ever imagined that the Guru's prophecy would come true.

SAVIOUR OF THE WORLD
GURU GOBIND SINGH

***Saviour of the world* -Guru Gobind Singh**

The painting by S. Trilok Singh Artist (1914-1990) has beautifully depicted Guru Gobind Singh, the founder of Khalsa Panth as the true saviour of human beings. The Guru succeeded in a seemingly impossible task.

The Tenth Guru completed the work of infusing courage, self-confidence, truthfulness, and bravery in the people, started by the first guru, Guru Nanak Dev.

For the Guru, all human beings are children of the same Almighty God. People rich or poor, belonging to different castes and creed are equal in the eyes of God. (ਹਿੰਦੂ ਤੁਰਕ ਕੋਊ ਰਾਫਜੀ ਇਮਾਮ ਸਾਫੀ ਮਾਨਸ ਕੀ ਜਾਤਿ ਸਬੈ ਏਕੈ ਪਹਿਚਾਨਬੋ।।)

He always believed that loving human beings is loving God. (ਸਾਚੁ ਕਹੋਂ ਸੁਨ ਲੇਹੁ ਸਭੈ ਜਿਨ ਪ੍ਰੇਮ ਕੀਓ ਤਿਨ ਹੀ ਪ੍ਰਭ ਪਾਇਓ।।)

The temple and the mosque are the same. Hindu worship and Muhammadon prayer are the same. People may follow different religions. They may go to a mosque or a temple. All religions are paths to the same one Supreme God. All men are equal.

The Guru always welcomed all who came to him, making no distinction between high and low, rich and poor, Hindus and Muslims. (ਦੇਹਰਾ ਮਸੀਤ ਸੋਈ ਪੂਜਾ ਔ ਨਿਵਾਜ ਉਈ ਮਾਨਸ ਸਬੈ ਏਕ ਪੈ ਅਨੇਕ ਕੋ ਭਰਮਾਉ ਹੈ)

People living in different places have their own set of beliefs. (ਦੇਵਤਾ ਅਦੇਵ ਜੱਛ ਗੰਧ੍ਰਬ ਤੁਰਕ ਹਿੰਦੂ ਨਿਆਰੇ ਨਿਆਰੇ ਦੇਸਨ ਕੇ ਭੇਸ ਕੋ ਪ੍ਰਭਾਉ ਹੈ।।) The Artist has shown that people belonging to different religions are the same.

In the painting, Guru Gobind Singh has been shown taking the ship towards its destination against all odds. He had to face many difficulties. Mughal forces were after him. Hill chiefs were always there to start the fight with him. The Guru worked for the upliftment and liberation of the downtrodden masses. Thus, annoying the religious leaders of both the Hindus and the Muslims. For helping his people, he gave everything. He sacrificed his father, sons, family, and friends for the love of his people.

People from different cultures, creed or beliefs are riding in the ship. But for the Guru, they are all children of God. 'Sarbat Da Bhala' (ਸਰਬੱਤ ਦਾ ਭਲਾ) wellness for everybody is written on the sail of the ship.

He always believed in truth and righteous actions above everything. He vowed to make the sparrow hunt and pluck the falcon, to make one fight a lakh and to make the poor and downtrodden become fearless brave saint-soldiers. He succeeded in a seemingly impossible task.

He is the true saviour of human beings. This has been beautifully depicted in the painting. The Artist has written Guru's message in Hindi, Punjabi, Bengali, and Urdu.

Today, our Guru does not need our head but wants us to spread the message of love for all, service towards others and unity among all. The artist has beautifully illustrated these messages in the painting.

REVIEWS ABOUT THE ARTIST

'Two Famous Sikh Artists' published in Deshmesh Edition of **'DESH DARPAN' Calcutta on 11-01-1935**

Sardar Trilok Singh ji (Jartauli) Artist Calcutta.
- Preparing portrait of Sant Attar Singh Mastuana.

Sardar Thakur Singh ji Artist
- paints a Bengali woman on canvas.

'The Khasi Hills Welsh Mission Hospital', SHILLONG, ASSAM. Dr. H. Gordon Robert, CMO and Robert Arthur Hughes, Sr. Medical Officer of HGR Hospital founded it in 1922. The Artist prepared one painting depicting Jesus Christ blessing the Hospital and gifted it to the Hospital on Christmas, when his son recovered. They sent a letter of appreciation.

'Ref.no 239 29th December 1941

Dear Mr. Trilok Singh,
Since I had the pleasure of receiving the gift, which you handed over on Christmas day. I have been able to study the painting more carefully. We all appreciate very greatly not only the beautiful gift but also the exceeding kindness which has inspired it. You have portrayed so beautifully on canvas, the work which the Hospital seeks to do and we are much moved by all that the picture reveals.

With renewed and warmest thanks and sharing with you the great satisfaction that you feel at your child's recovery.'

Yours sincerely,
Dr. H. G. Roberts
Welsh Presbyterian Mission

Bhai Sahib Bhai Randhir Singh, Narangwal 1944

S.Trilok Singh completed the painting on the life of Guru Nanak in 1944 in Assam after thorough study of the history of Guru Nanak. He shifted to his Vill. Jartauli P.O. Kila Raipur in 1944. Bhai Sahib Randhir Singh was very much impressed with this painting and wanted to get it published. Due to Second World War, the painting could not be printed in German print. Bhai sahib said, "Don't sell this painting or give as gift and keep faith in Almighty. Almighty will take this service Himself." This painting is still displayed in 'Chitralok', Patiala.

ਕਲਾ ਜ਼ੌਹਰੀ ਤੇ ਕਰਮ ਯੋਗੀ **Sri Swami Keshwa Nand, Sangaria (Raj) 1954**

Sri Swami was Member Parliament at the time of PEPSU. He visited S. Trilok Singh Artist and was impressed with the Gurbani illustrations and other paintings. He purchased 33 paintings of the artist in 1952-53. These paintings were displayed in a room named 'Trilok Kala Kaksh' in his museum at Sangaria (Rajisthan). The Artist was honoured in annual function held at Sangaria in 1954.

Dr. Ganda Singh MA Ph.D Director, Punjabi Mehkma and Archives Deptt. PEPSU, Patiala wrote about the Artist

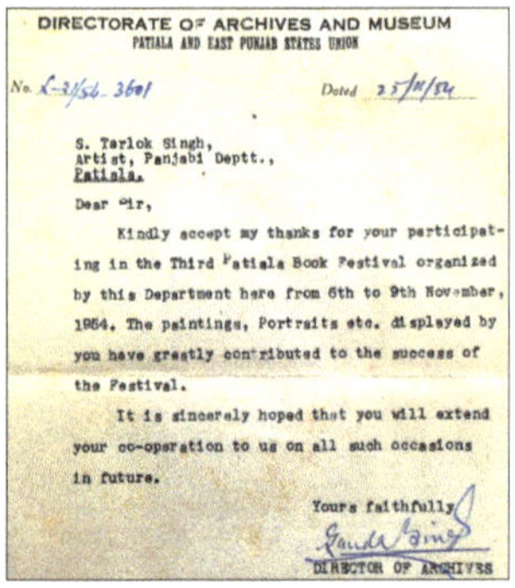

DIRECTORATE OF ARCHIVES AND MUSEUM
PATIALA AND EAST PUNJAB STATES UNION

No. L-21/56-3601 Dated 25/11/54

S. Tarlok Singh,
Artist, Panjabi Deptt.,
Patiala.

Dear Sir,

Kindly accept my thanks for your participating in the Third Patiala Book Festival organized by this Department here from 6th to 9th November, 1954. The paintings, Portraits etc. displayed by you have greatly contributed to the success of the Festival.

It is sincerely hoped that you will extend your co-operation to us on all such occasions in future.

Yours faithfully,
Ganda Singh
DIRECTOR OF ARCHIVES

Artist Trilok Singh prepared pages having four columns for block printing of four volumes of rare *Mahan Kosh* (Encyclopedia of Sikh Literature) of Bhai Kahan Singh of Nabha published in 1935 to make one volume. This work was given to the Artist by the Director, Punjabi Mehkma & Archives in 1954. With the merger of PEPSU in Punjab, the name changed to Language Deptt., Punjab. Later it was published in 1960. This is now a reference volume.

'ਅਣਕੱਟ ਹੀਰਾ

ਪਹਿਲਾ ਕੰਮ ਜੋ ਸਰਦਾਰ ਤ੍ਰਿਲੋਕ ਸਿੰਘ ਚਿਤ੍ਰਕਾਰ ਜੀ ਦੇ ਸਪੁਰਦ ਕੀਤਾ ਗਿਆ ਉਹ ਸੀ ਭਾਈ ਕਾਨ੍ਹ ਸਿੰਘ ਜੀ ਦੇ ਚਾਰ ਜਿਲਦਾਂ ਵਿਚ ਸਰਕਾਰ ਪਟਿਆਲਾ ਵਲੋਂ ਛਾਪੇ ਹੋਏ ਦੁਰਲਭ ਮਹਾਨ ਕੋਸ਼ ਨੂੰ ਇਕ ਜਿਲਦ ਵਿਚ ਛਪਵਾਉਣ ਲਈ ਖਰੜਾ ਤਿਆਰ ਕਰਨਾ। ਚੌਂਹ ਸਫਿਆਂ ਨੂੰ ਇਕ ਸਫੇ ਵਿਚ ਕਿਵੇਂ ਸਮੋਣਾ ਹੈ ਇਹ ਵਿਉਂਤ ਤਾਂ ਮੈਂ ਬਣਾ ਕੇ ਮਹਿਕਮੇ ਲਈ, ਸਰਕਾਰ ਦੀ ਉੱਚ ਪੱਧਰੀ ਕਮੇਟੀ ਪਾਸੋਂ, ਜਿਸ ਦੇ ਪਰਧਾਨ ਸ; ਬ; ਸਰਦਾਰ ਮੋਹਨ ਸਿੰਘ ਜੀ, ਚੇਅਰਮੈਨ ਪਬਿਲਕ ਸਰਵਿਸ ਕਮਿਸ਼ਨ ਸਨ, ਪ੍ਰਵਾਨ ਕਰਵਾ ਲਈ ਸੀ, ਪਰ ਜਿਸ ਸੁਚੱਜੇ ਢੰਗ ਅਤੇ ਜਾਨਮਾਰੀ ਨਾਲ ਤ੍ਰਿਲੋਕ ਸਿੰਘ ਜੀ ਨੇ ਉਸ ਵਿਉਂਤ ਅਨੁਸਾਰ ਇਹ ਖਰੜਾ ਤਿਆਰ ਕੀਤਾ ਅਤੇ ਸਾਫ ਸੁਥਰੀ ਛਪਾਈ ਯੋਗ ਬਣਾਇਆ, ਉਸ ਲਈ ਮਹਿਕਮਾ ਹੀ ਨਹੀਂ ਬਲਕਿ ਮਹਾਨ ਕੋਸ਼ ਤੋਂ ਲਾਭ ਲੈਣ ਵਾਲੇ ਸਾਰੇ ਇਨ੍ਹਾਂ ਦੇ ਧੰਨਵਾਦੀ ਰਹਿਣਗੇ।'

Dr. Ganda Singh

The *Mahan Kosh* (Encyclopedia of Sikh Literature) of Bhai Kahan Singh of Nabha was published in 1960 in one volume for the first time. In the preface of the Mahan Kosh, Giani Lal Singh, Director, Language Department, Punjab has also appreciated the work done by Artist Trilok Singh.

ਮੁੱਖ ਸ਼ਬਦ

"ਇਸ ਸਬੰਧ ਵਿੱਚ ਗਵਰਨਮੈਂਟ ਆਫ਼ ਇੰਡਿਆ ਦੇਹਰਾਦੂਨ (ਯੂ ਪੀ) ਦਾ ਪ੍ਰਬੰਧ ਕੀਤਾ ਗਿਆ ਤੇ ਇਸੇ ਪ੍ਰੈਸ ਰਾਹੀਂ ਅਮਰੀਕਾ ਦੀ ਇਕ ਫਰਮ ਦਾ ਵਧੀਆ ਕਾਗਜ ਖਰੀਦਿਆ ਗਿਆ। ਇਸ ਤਰਾਂ ਪ੍ਰਬੰਧ ਹੋਣ ਤੇ 1954 ਵਿੱਚ ਫੋਟੋ ਬਲਾਕਾਂ ਦੀ ਛਪਾਈ ਸ਼ੁਰੂ ਹੋਈ।

ਸ੍ਰੀ ਤਰਲੋਕ ਸਿੰਘ ਚਿਤਰਕਾਰ ਤੇ ਸ੍ਰੀ ਗੋਬਿੰਦ ਸਿੰਘ ਜਿੰਨ੍ਹਾਂ ਨੇ ਫੋਟੋਜ਼ ਲਈ ਪਤਰਿਆ ਨੂੰ ਬਣਾਇਆ ਤੇ ਸਵਾਰਿਆ ਵੀ ਪ੍ਰਸ਼ੰਸਾਂ ਦੇ ਹਕਦਾਰ ਹਨ।.."

ਲਾਲ ਸਿੰਘ ਡਾਇਰੈਕਟਰ
ਭਾਸ਼ਾ ਵਿਭਾਗ ਪੰਜਾਬ, ਪਟਿਆਲਾ। **1960**

Punjab Govt. organised a special state level functionon 25-11-1973 at Chitralok Patiala, Chief Minister, Punjab, Giani Zail Singh honoured the Artist and inaugurated painting exhibition of the Artist.

The photo is of the inauguration of the Exhibition. Left to Right are - Wing Commander S. Atma Singh Lotay, the Chief Minister Punjab, S. GS Panchhi, the Artist, S. Bishan Singh Rehal and S. Jaiteg Singh Anant.

ਗਿਆਨੀ ਜ਼ੈਲ ਸਿੰਘ ਦੇ ਦੋ ਸ਼ਬਦ ਚਿਤਰਕਾਰ ਨੂੰ ਭੇਂਟ

'ਸ੍ਰ ਤਿਰਲੋਕ ਸਿੰਘ ਚਿੱਤਰਕਾਰ ਜੀ ਦੀ ਪ੍ਰਦਰਸ਼ਨੀ ਨੂੰ ਦੇਖ ਕੇ ਪ੍ਰਸੰਨਤਾ ਹੋਈ। ਨਹਾਇਤ ਹੀ ਬਰੀਕੀ ਤੇ ਪੁਰਾਤਨ ਵ ਵਰਤਮਾਨ ਇਤਿਹਾਸਕ ਘਟਨਾਵਾਂ ਨੂੰ ਚਿੱਤਰਕੇ ਨਵਾਂ ਰਸਤਾ ਬਨਾਇਆ।

ਚਿੱਤਰਾਂ ਦੇ ਨਾਲ ਖਿਆਲਾਂ ਦਾ ਪ੍ਰਗਟਾਵਾ ਤੇ ਹਾਲਾਤ ਦੇ ਦਰਿਸ਼ ਦੇਖ ਕੇ ਜਿਵੇਂ ਚਿੱਤਰਕਾਰੀ ਦੇ ਕੰਮ ਵਿਚ ਉਹਨਾਂ ਨੇ ਵਿਸ਼ੇਸ਼ ਥਾਂ ਬਣਾਈ ਹੈ।

ਮੇਰੀ ਕਾਮਨਾ ਹੈ ਕਿ ਚਿੱਤਰਕਾਰ ਦੀ ਉਮਰ ਲੰਮੀ, ਸੇਹਤਵੰਦ ਜਿੰਦਗੀ ਰਹੇ ਤੇ ਉਹ ਹੋਰ ਵੀ ਸੇਵਾ ਕਰ ਸਕਣ।'

ਜ਼ੈਲ ਸਿੰਘ, CM,

A letter of Sardar Sobha Singh Artist, Andretta (HP) dated
15-09-1974

'ਅੱਜ ਕਲ੍ਹ ਦੇ ਕਈ ਕਲਾਕਾਰਾਂ ਨੂੰ ਵੇਖ ਕੇ ਸ਼ਰਮ ਆਉਂਦੀ ਹੈ ਪਰ ਅਪਣੀ ਸ਼ਖਸੀਅਤ ਅਪਣੀ ਕਲਾ ਵਰਗੀ ਬਣਾ ਲੈਣੀ ਆਪ ਦੀ ਕਮਾਈ ਦਾ ਕਮਾਲ ਹੈ। ਮੈਨੂੰ ਆਪ ਦੀ ਮਿੱਤ੍ਰਤਾ ਤੇ ਸ਼੍ਰੇਣੀ ਚ ਹੋਣ ਦਾ ਬੜਾ ਮਾਣ ਤੇ ਗੌਰਵ ਹੈ। ਸਿੱਖੀ ਸਿਦਕ, ਗੁਰਬਾਣੀ ਦਾ ਪਿਆਰ, ਨਿਮਰਤਾ, ਉਚੱਾ ਆਚਾਰ ਤੇ ਡੁਲਦਾ ਪਿਆਰ ਆਪ ਦੇ ਹਿੱਸੇ ਹੀ ਆਯਾ ਹੈ। ਆਪ ਦੀ ਕਲਾ ਦਾ ਆਦ੍ਰਸ਼ :- ਸਿੱਖ ਇਤਿਹਾਸ ਤੇ ਗੁਰਬਾਣੀ ਨੂੰ ਸਾਕਾਰ ਕਰਨ ਦੀ ਲਗਣ ਵੇਖ ਕੇ ਸਿਰ ਸ਼ਰਧਾ ਨਾਲ ਝੁਕ ਜਾਂਦਾ ਹੈ। ਪ੍ਰਮਾਤਮਾ ਆਪ ਦੀ ਕਮਾਈ ਚ ਬਰਕਤ ਪਾਉਣ ਅਤੇ ਆਪ ਦੀ ਕਲਾ ਕਮਾਈ ਦੀ ਘਾਲਣਾ ਨੂੰ ਸਫਲ ਕਰਨ, ਮੇਰੀ ਇਹੀ ਦਿਲੀ ਅਰਦਾਸ ਹੈ।'

ਆਪ ਦਾ ਸਨੇਹੀ-ਸੋਭਾ ਸਿੰਘ

The President, SGPC, Amritsar honoured the Artist in
1977-78

400th anniversary of Amritsar foundation day was celebrated by SGPC, Amritsar in 1977-78 and the oil painting on the life of Guru Gobind Singh depicted in nineteen stars was chosen as the best one. President, SGPC, Amritsar S. GS Tohra honoured Artist Trilok Singh with a "Siropa" and cash award. This oil painting was kept by the SGPC, Amritsar with assurance to print for distribution. The original oil painting is with SGPC.

American Singhs visited 'Chitralok' Patiala **18.10.1979**

Letter of Appreciation

'On October 18, 1979, we visited Gurmat Art Gallery of S. Trilok Singh Artist at Patiala. For all of us, this was our first time experience of the scope and magnitude of his work. What captured people's heart and minds most was how over and over again Sardar Trilok Singh could bring alive in paintings greater power of different concepts, principles and supreme mystical truth of Sikhism. Intangible as courage, sacrifice, meditative bliss, peace etc... were rendered into the paintings with such dynamic inspiration that all were again and again moved and uplifted. Karmjit Singh finally hustled us away to meet the tight schedule with great difficulty. Most of us were keen on finding out how some of the paintings or possible reproductions could be obtained as Guru has willed, this will have to wait until another time but just knowing this collection of inspiring works is a happy thought indeed.'

Wahe Guru Ji Ka Khalsa, Wahe Guru Ji Fateh,
S. Marn Sumat Singh, Washington, DC, USA

Language department of Punjab, published book on the Artist and released it on 70th birthday of the Artist on **10/12/1984**

Language Deptt., Punjab organised a special function on 70th birthday of S. Trilok Singh in Central Library, Patiala and inaugurated exhibition of paintings of the Artist and honoured the Artist by releasing a book published by Language Deptt., Punjab.

The book titled '**Chitralok's contribution to Art**' is on the life, works of the Artist and his contribution to Art. The Chitralok is the name of the residence of the Artist. This book was written by Dr. Saroj Pandhey (Dr. Saroj Chaman), Punjabi University, Patiala published by Language Deptt., Patiala. S. Kapur Singh Ghuman was the Director of the Department at that time.

A documentary film

"Great Master of North Zone
S. Trilok Singh Artist
-- an Eminent Chitarkar"

North Zone Cultural Center,
Govt. of India
1995

North Zone Culture Center, Govt. of India
1995

Prepared a documentary film on late S. Trilok Singh Artist, 'Chitralok', Patiala in 1995 under heading "Great Master of North Zone, S. Trilok Singh Artist - an Eminent Chitarkar".

Dr. Saroj Sharma, Director, Museum & Art Gallery, Faculty of Fine Arts & Culture, Punjabi University, Patiala after lot of research work, was awarded Ph.D in Fine Arts "ART OF TRILOK SINGH" in September, 2001.

A Spiritual Glow

The paintings of S. Trilok Singh are precious pages of the history. These compositions are drenched in religious fervor and constitute elements of a language adequate to articulate his emotions through media of form and colour. Being religion oriented artist he selected verses from Sri Guru Granth Sahib ji and translated precepts into manifestations of colour visions. It is presentation of a perfect match of thought, vision and skill. These paintings are based on spiritual poetry and he has communicated the 'DIVINE WORLD' in a spirit of deep humanity and compassion for mankind. The spirit of Ten Gurus enshrined in these paintings. The teachings of the Sikh religion is to uplift the society. The uniqueness of event show artist's strong power of visualisation. The artist acts as God's spy to convey the superb actions could only originate pure thoughts ...

Dr. Saroj Sharma

Dr. Saroj Sharma, Director, Museum and art Gallery,
Punjabi University, Patiala

Punjabi University, Patiala organised a special function to set up 'S. Trilok Singh Artist Gold Medal' for awarding the medal to the topper of MA, Fine Arts.
17-04-2004

"I had honour to introduce S. Trilok Singh Medal in 2005 for the best student of Fine Arts Department, Punjabi University, Patiala. According to my opinion, the artistic worth of these paintings is at par with the literary merits of verses of Gurbani."

Swarn Singh Boparai,
Vice Chancellor, Punjabi University, Patiala

S. Swarn Singh Boparai, Kirti Chakra, Padama Shri (Awardee)

Vice Chancellor, Punjabi University, Patiala inaugurated an exhibition of paintings by late S. Trilok Singh named '**A SPRITUAL GLOW**' in Museum and Art Gallery, Punjabi University, Patiala **19-06-2006 to 22-06-2006**

"From the galaxy of traditional Sikh painters of Punjab, It seems S. Trilok Singh was endowed with rare power of imagination and observation. He had the faith that only Guru could liberate the man. He took as a moral duty to inspire men through his paintings to follow the path shown by the Gurus. A message is hidden in paintings like fragrance in flowers."

S. Swarn Singh Boparai
Vice Chancellor, Punjabi University, Patiala

Department of Tourism, Govt. of Bihar
September 2016

Bihar Tourism gave befitting tribute in celebrating with pride 350th Prakash Purv to Sri Guru Gobind Singh. Bihar Tourism released books in Punjabi and English on his life and times and places consecrated by Tenth Sikh Guru, titled 'Sarbans Dani Deshmesh Pita Shri Guru Gobind Singh ji Maharaj, 350th Prakash Parv'.

Bihar Tourism included the works of S. Trilok Singh Artist with acknowledgment to- *Jotinder Singh, Engineer-in-Chief/PSEB /Retd, 'Chitralok', Patiala. (www.triloksinghartist.com)*

BIHAR TOURISM
Blissful Bihar

Punjabi University, Patiala organised an exhibition of paintings by Artist S. Trilok Singh, on the life and teachings of Guru Nanak from 13th to 20 th August, 2019 on 550 th. Parkash Purv of Guru Nanak Dev ji. The University has published the catalogue about the Artist. Dr. BS Ghuman, VC, Pbi. University has released the catalogue in honour of the Artist.

Chardikala newspaper published two page coloured supplement on 13th. August having articles/messages about the Artist by Sikh Scholars and writers S. Jaiteg Singh Anant, founder Trustee, Hardarshan Memorial International Trust, Canada, S. Tarlochan Singh Ex-MP and Ex-Chairman, minorities commission, Prof. Balkar Singh Director, World Punjabi Center, Dr. BS Ghuman VC, Pbi. University, Dr. Gurmit Singh, Prof. Incharge Guru Gobind Singh Chair, Pbi. University, Patiala and S. Jagjit Singh Dardi, Chairman, Charhdikala Group.

A book was published in 1974 in Punjabi "BANGLA DE DAAB". Artcles in the book were translated by S. Trilok Singh Artist from Bengali to Punjabi. The Book has beautiful literary stories and essays.

The book "Duna Laha" was written and published by the Artist in 1987. This book contains articles written by the Artist and the articles about the Artist.

The Artist used to design the title pages of monthly magazines PUNJABI DUNIYA, SAPT SINDHU, JAN SAHIT and books published by Punjabi Mehkma and Language Department Punjab.

Artist Trilok Singh's remarkable contribution to Punjabi Encyclopedia.

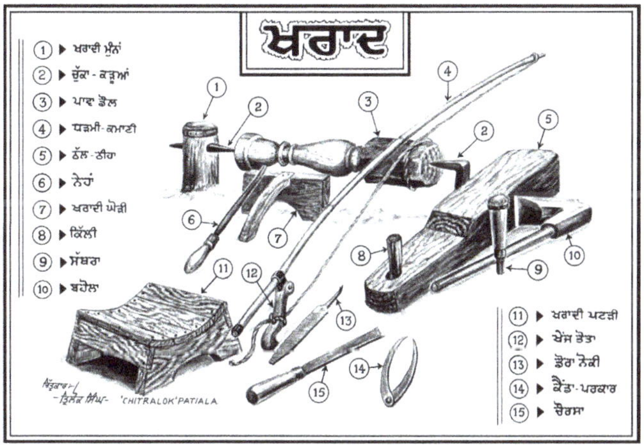

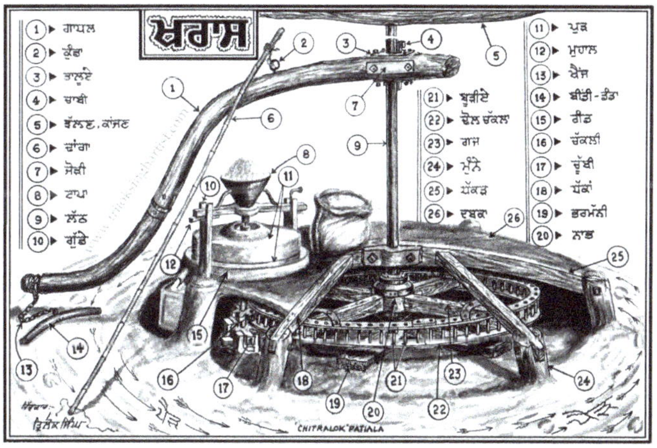

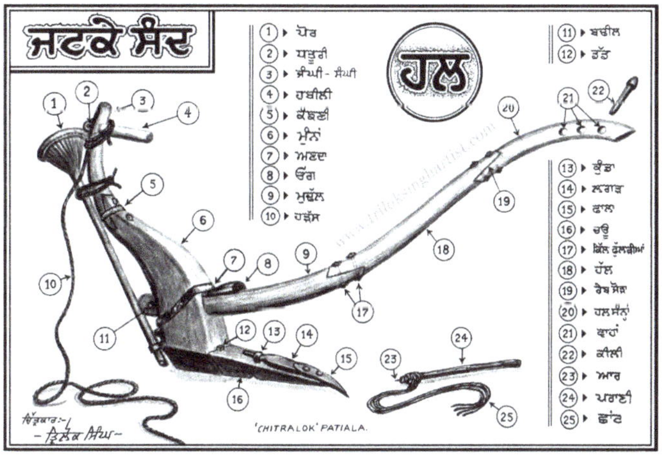

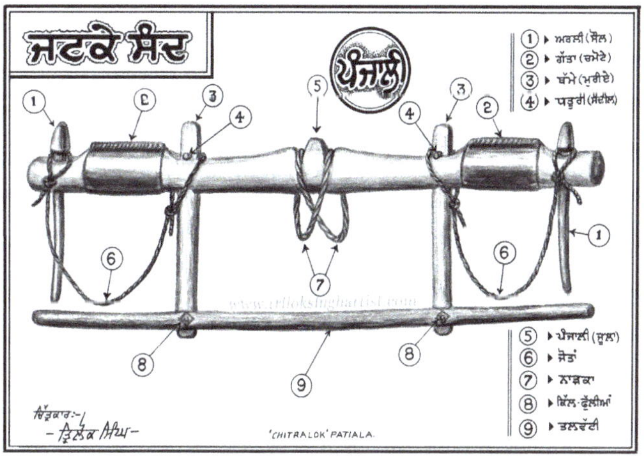

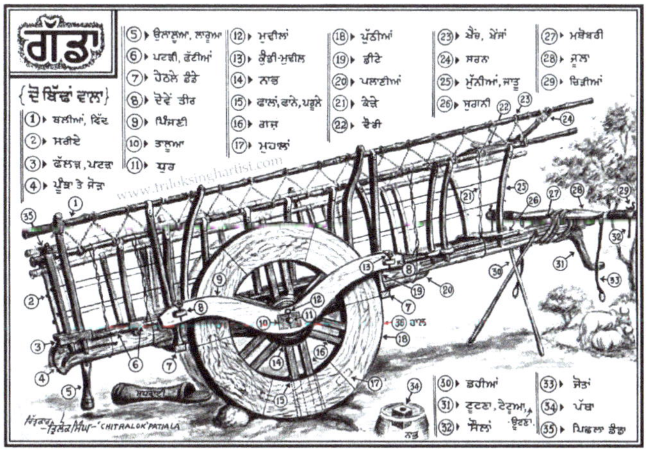

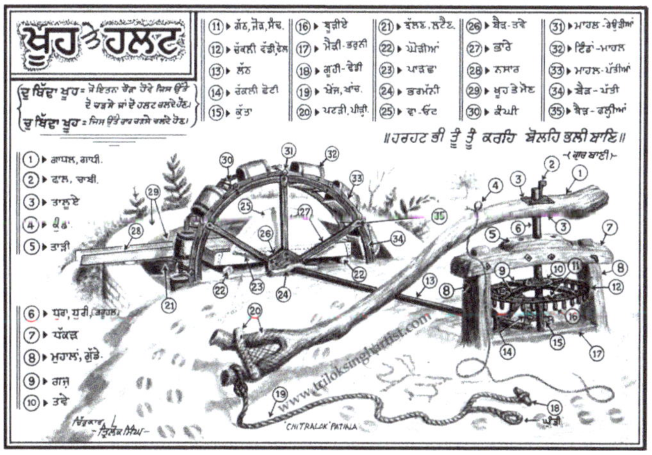

ਖਾਲਸਾ ਮੇਰੋ ਰੂਪ ਹੈ ਖਾਸ। ਖਾਲਸਾ ਮਹਿ ਹਉ ਕਰਉ ਨਿਵਾਸ।..
ਖਾਲਸਾ ਮੇਰੋ ਪਿੰਡ ਪਰਾਨ। ਖਾਲਸਾ ਮੇਰੀ ਜਾਨ ਕੀ ਜਾਨ।..
ਖਾਲਸਾ ਮੇਰੋ ਸਤਿਗੁਰ ਪੂਰਾ। ਖਾਲਸਾ ਮੇਰੋ ਸਜਨ ਸੂਰਾ।..
ਯਾ ਮੈ ਰੰਚ ਨਾ ਮਿਥਿਆ ਭਾਖੀ। ਪਾਰਬ੍ਰਹਮ ਗੁਰੂ ਨਾਨਕ ਸਾਖੀ॥..

ਜਬ ਲਗ ਖਾਲਸਾ ਰਹੇ ਨਿਆਰਾ। ਤਬ ਲਗ ਤੇਜ ਕੀਉ ਮੈ ਸਾਰਾ।
ਜਬ ਇਹ ਗਹੈ ਬਿਪਰਨ ਕੀ ਰੀਤ। ਮੈ ਨ ਕਰੋ ਇਨ ਕੀ ਪਰਤੀਤ॥

Khalsa is my true form. Within the Khalsa, I abide.
Khalsa is my body & soul. Khalsa is the breath of my life.
Khalsa is my complete true Guru. Khalsa is my fearless partner.
I have not told you even a lie. Perfect saint Guru Nanak is my witness.

While the Khalsa stays true. I will be with them.
When Khalsa does not stay true. I will not stand with them.

–Guru Gobind Singh - Khalsa Mahima

S. TRILOK SINGH ARTIST
(10-12-1914 TO 11-12-1990)

Artist Trilok Singh was born in village Jartauli, district Ludhiana, Punjab. His father S. Gurdit Singh was a Railway engineer, who worked in Uganda, South Africa, and Assam. His mother died when he was five years old. His father left him in the care of his grandfather who was well conversant with Gurbani, being a Sikh devout. So the Artist developed great interest in Gurbani from a very early age. After the death of his grandfather, his father took him to Assam. On seeing his interest in painting, he sent him to Calcutta to receive training from Artist SG Thakur Singh. He always felt obliged to his grandfather for moulding him. He established his career as an Artist in Calcutta. After the death of his father in Assam, he shifted back to his native place. After independence, he joined as State Artist, Patiala, then Mehkma Punjabi, now Language Dept. Punjab.

The Artist was honoured in 1973 by Chief Minister, Punjab, Giani Zail Singh in a State-level function organised at his residence - 'Chitralok', Patiala.

He had great interest in Gurbani, history and culture, and was proficient in many languages - Punjabi, Hindi, Urdu, English, Persian, Bengali, and Assamese. He developed his unique style of illustrating Gurbani shabads, folklore, history, culture, social evils, nature, and visuals in Punjabi encyclopedia. He translated number of Bengali articles in Punjabi and published them in the book named 'Bangla De Daab'.

He is the first Punjabi Artist, on whose works 'Art of S. Trilok Singh', Ph.D. has been awarded by Punjabi University, Patiala, posthumously.

A gold medal in the name of the Artist has been established by Punjabi University, Patiala and is awarded to the topper of M.A. Fine Arts.

1935
Calcutta

1953
Patiala

1973
Patiala

9-12-1990
Patiala

Gurmukhi script used by the Tenth Guru and the present day.

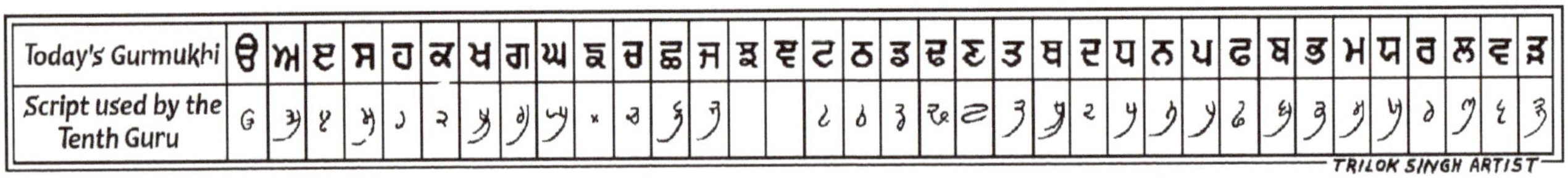

Artist S. Trilok Singh prepared the developmant of Gurmukhi script from 375 AD to present day.
This was published by Language departnent, Punjab.

ਗੁਰਮੁਖੀ ਦਾ ਵਿਕਾਸ

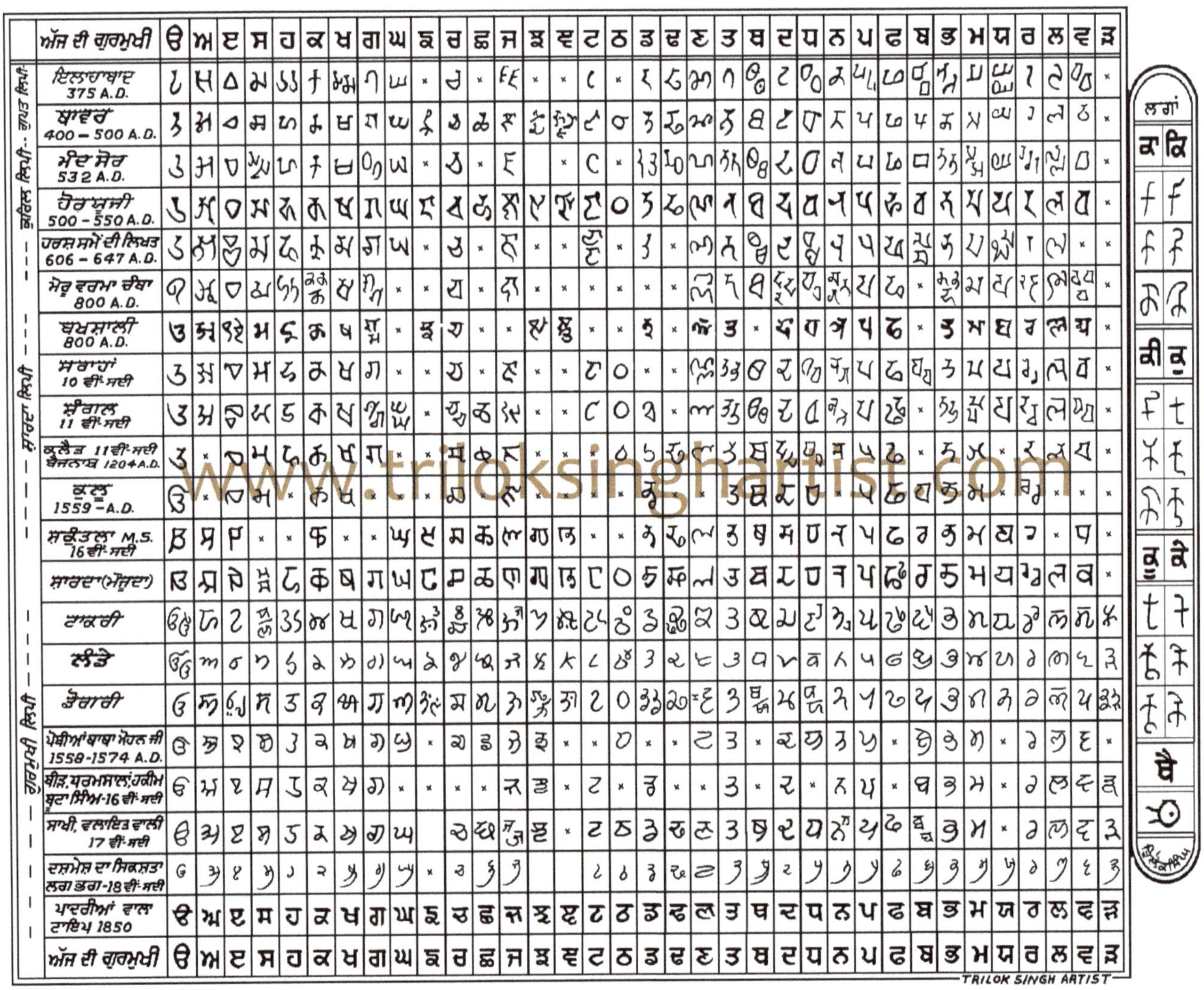

www.ingramcontent.com/pod-product-compliance
Ingram Content Group UK Ltd.
Pitfield, Milton Keynes, MK11 3LW, UK
UKHW060120010826
14089UKWH00005B/84